E. V. B.

Days and Hours in a Garden

E. V. B.

Days and Hours in a Garden

ISBN/EAN: 9783337069889

Printed in Europe, USA, Canada, Australia, Japan

Cover: Foto ©Andreas Hilbeck / pixelio.de

More available books at **www.hansebooks.com**

DAYS AND HOURS IN A GARDEN.

Dec. 22 We go tomorrow — till
Faringford
Tuesday

Dearest Lady Arthur

If you have not got
these, will you love them,
or some, for my sake? That
Poet is such a joy to me —
I have not written name, in
Case you have it — (or hate it)
If either, let me exchange it —
With loving wishes yr
affectionate Eleanor Vere Boyle

At the South Window.

DAYS AND HOURS IN A GARDEN.

BY

"E. V. B."

"God Almighty first planted a garden;
And indeed it is the purest of human pleasures."

BACON.

NINTH EDITION.

LONDON:
ELLIOT STOCK, 62, PATERNOSTER ROW, E.C.
1896.

NOS ET MEDITEMUR IN HORTO

TO

RICHARD CAVENDISH BOYLE.

WHOSE LOVE FOR NATURE AND FOR ART,

YEARS HAD NOT CHILLED

NOR TROUBLE CHANGED,

THESE RECORDS OF OUR GARDEN

WERE INSCRIBED BY

E. V. B.,

IN 1884.

PREFACE.

IF for a sixth reprint of DAYS AND HOURS
IN A GARDEN a new Preface was deemed
advisable, still more so, perhaps, should
there be something new prefixed to the Seventh
Edition, although, indeed, it contains nothing
that in any sense is new. Neither new words
nor any new vignettes appear therein. Nevertheless we venture to hope that perhaps new
readers may be found. Since the last edition
was published some three years have come
and gone, with their world-old roll of seasons
and their burden of inevitable change. The
garden has three times slept beneath the rains
and the snows of winter, and has awakened in
spring with the birds and the bees. Meanwhile, the shrubs are taller and larger, and the
trees have extended their roots and stretched
out their branches over lawns and gravel paths.
And the summer shade, so coveted in other

days, has broadened, while, on the other hand,
it has become more hard to maintain in their
wonted brilliancy our borders and flowerful
closes. The axe and the pruning-knife have
been busy during the winter months; and many
a fine Laurel, in all its wealth of glossy green,
has been laid low, and with Yew and the full-
foliaged Phylleria, and more than one tall Deodara,—become a burnt sacrifice to "Apollo's
sunny ray." For the south sunshine must be
let in, no matter what the cost. In certain
ways the garden may be said to *suffer* change;
and chiefly when the grace and softly rounded
loveliness of various evergreens which do not
bear the shears—Cryptomeria Elegans, Red
Cedar, and the like—after a course of years
begins to wane. Even to the upward-pointing
Cypress middle life in an English garden is
not becoming. And as the larger trees increase
in size, so the overshadowed lawns diminish.
And thus the slower progress of some of our
trees has given place to a rapid growth, which
bids fair to overstep all bounds of such limited
space as ours. The Douglas Fir and the
branching Cedar of Lebanon keep growing
into one another, while Excelsa touches them
both, and wants to reach across to the clump
of Yew and Laburnum. Their near neighbour
the Sequoia already rises to the height of fifty

feet, and measures over nine feet round at
some two feet from the ground. Nordmaniana
alone (most beautiful of all), through having
five times lost his leader, is forced to greater
moderation. Still, although no future of green
maturity can ever compensate the earlier, ex-
pectant delight of watching our young trees'
youth, all is not lost; for the pleasures carried
away by Time, Time itself replaces by others
to the full as sweet. It may be that favourite
plants become established and yield a larger
harvest of beauty, or that deep-laid plans ripen
into bright perfection, while a thousand garden
joys arise fresh each year, nay, well-nigh every
day. As to the living frequenters of the garden,
whose presence there for the most part en-
hances our enjoyment of it, the tomtits and
nuthatches, are as busy with the cocoanuts
which hang for their use all winter from the
Rose-arches as the mice and the sparrows are
with the crocuses; the white pigeons still circle
in the air and settle upon the gables, or preen
their feathers in the sunshine amongst the
yellow stonecrop at the base of the old grey
pillar in the parterr; the swallows return year
by year to their nests within the porch; but the
faithful satin-coated Collie lies still for ever
under the turf by the ivied wall, and the earth
lies heavy on his noble head. For these thirteen

summers past he had taken his pleasure in
the garden—had chased marauding cats, or
bounded after apples with any playfellow of the
hour, while his glad bark rang again; or as
in later days, had gravely followed the steps
of his mistress about the walks, or rolled upon
the grass, or watched with lazy but unfailing
interest his friend the Gardener at work. Four
words graven on a little white marble tablet
that shines amidst the dark ivy-leaves on the
wall record his name and character :—

CASSIO.

TENDER AND TRUE.

May, 1876.]   [*Nov.*, 1889.

Already the Snowdrops are giving way before
impatient Hepaticas and Primroses, the bare
Elms are thickening with purple, and we begin
to count the Gentian buds. Everywhere Nature
repairs herself in ceaseless round. Only in
our human lives some vacant spots there may
be, where the grass will not grow green again.

E. V. B.

Huntercombe Manor,
February, 1890

OCTOBER.

I

Fas est hic, Indulgere Genio.

I.

OCTOBER 17, 1882.

Of Nuns and White Owls ; Yews, Thrushes, and Nut-crackers.

THE GARDEN'S STORY. It is only eleven years old, though the place itself is an old place—an old place without a history, for scarce a record remains of it anywhere that we have ever found. Its name occurs on a headstone in the parish churchyard, and on one or two monuments within the chancel of the parish church. There is brief mention of it in Evelyn's *Diary*. It is there described as "a very pretty seate in the forest, on a flat, with gardens exquisitely kept, tho' large, and the house, a staunch good old building." It seems George Evelyn (the author's cousin) was amongst the many who have lived here once. At that time eighty acres of wood

surrounded the house, where now there lies
a treeless stretch of flat cornfields. Quite
near, across the road, are the ruins of an
ancient nunnery. Our meadow under the
high convent wall is called the Walk Meadow, because here the nuns used to walk.
The great Walnut tree, which they might
possibly have known, only died after we
came. It was cut down for firewood, and
its hollows were full of big chestnut-coloured
"rat bats," very fierce and strong. At that
time also white owls lived in the ruins,
and used to come floating over the lawn at
twilight—until the days of gun licenses,
since when, they have disappeared. Dim
legends surround the place, but nothing
clear or certain is known or even said, and
there is not a ghost anywhere. All we know
is, that since taking possession, wherever a
hole is dug in the garden to plant a tree, the
spade is sure to strike against some old
brick foundation of such firm construction
that they have to use the pick to break it up.
Bones of large dogs also are found all about
the place whenever the ground is broken—
remains of the watch dogs, or hunting dogs,

of the olden time—also quaintly shaped
tobacco-pipes. I know of nothing to sup-
port the tradition that monks abode here
once. There were signs of an upstairs room
having at some remote time been used as a
chapel; a piscina in the wall and a narrow
lancet window having been found and
destroyed, when the house was in the
builder's hands eleven years ago. Broken
arches, also, and mouldings in chalk and
stone, were dug up out of the foundations of
some outhouses at the same time. "They
say" there is an underground passage between the Abbey and the house, but we do
not believe it, and we do not believe in
the murder of a monk for his money, said
to have been committed by a nun in the
upper room now a guest-chamber. Such
vague traditions are sure to hang around
old walls, like mists about a damp meadow.
Very distinct, however, and carved in no
vague characters, are certain initials and
dates still visible on the stems of the trees
in the Lime avenue. For in old times—

"Fond lovers, cruel as their flame,
    Cut in these trees their mistress' name."

When the trees are bare and the western sky
is bright, you can see them quite plainly—
large capital letters, often a pair, enclosed in
a large heart with the date. The dates run
from 1668 on to late in 1700. Those old
village lovers must have had sharp pen-knives,
which cut deep! They and their names have
long passed away and been forgotten; but,
for so much as is traced in the living bark,
these Limes have proved as good as any
marble monument; much better than the
long wooden "rails" which are still in
fashion hereabouts. Since the place was
ours this short avenue of twenty-four trees
has been taken in from the public road; and
now the Limes give us cool shade and fragrance and many midges in the hot summer
days. I fear there is nothing more to be
discovered about the past history of the
House than we now already know. We
must be content, and follow as we best may
George Herbert's concise admonition—

> " When you chance for to find
> An old house to your mind,
> Be good to the poor,
> As God gives you store."

We have had the great pleasure of making
the garden. The feature of the place was,
and is, two symmetrically planted groups of
magnificent Elms in the park field, in which
every season we hope the rooks will build.
There was everything to be done in the
garden, to which these Elms form a background. We found hardly any flowers; a
large square lawn laid out in beds, with unsatisfactory turf and shrubberies beyond, a
long, broad terrace walk, old brick walls,
with stone balls on the corners, two or three
old wrought iron gates in the wrong places,
dabs of kitchen garden and potato plots,
stable-yard and carriage entrance occupying
the whole south front, with a few pleasant
trees, a young Wellingtonia, a Stone Pine, a
Venetian Sumach (*Rhus cotinus*), and a very
large red Chestnut (from a seed brought from
Spain in the waistcoat pocket of one of our
predecessors here, fifty years ago, and said
to be the first of the kind raised in England).
Such was our new playground in 1871.
Here we brought a skilful Gardener, possessed
of common sense and uncommon good taste
—can one say much more in a few words?

—and aided by our own most unscientific but exceeding love for flowers and gardening, we set to work at once. These " gardens on a flat " are transformed.

There now are close-trimmed Yew hedges, some of those first planted being 8 feet 6 inches high, and nearly 3 feet through, while others are kept low and square. There are Yews cut in pyramids and buttresses against the walls, and Yews in every stage of natural growth. I love the English Yew, with its "thousand years of gloom!" (an age that ours, however, have not yet attained). The Wellingtonia, planted in 1866, has shot up to over forty feet high, and far outgrown its youthful Jack-in-the-Green look. The Stone Pine, alas! has split in two, and been propped up; and although half killed since by frost, it yet bears a yearly harvest of fine cones, chiefly collected for use as fire revivers— though the seeds ripen for sowing, or eating. The borders are filled with the dearest old-fashioned plants; the main entrance is removed to the north side; the stable-yard is removed also, and instead thereof are turf and straight walks, and a sun-dial, and a

Kitchen Garden, East Lawn, etc.

parterre for bedding-out things—the sole
plot allowed here for scarlet Pelargoniums
and the like. In this parterre occurs the only
foliage plant we tolerate—a deep crimson
velvet-leaved Coleus. The centre bed is a
raised square of yellow Stonecrop and little
white Harebells; with an old stone pedestal,
found in a stonemason's yard, bearing a leaden
inscription—"to Deborah"—surmounted
by a ball, on which the white pigeons
picturesquely perch. There are green walks
between Yew hedges and flower borders,
Beech hedges, and a long green tunnel—the
Allée Verte—so named in remembrance of a
bower-walk in an old family place, no longer
in existence. There are nooks and corners,
and a grand, well-shaded tennis-lawn, and
crown of all, there is the "Fantaisie"! This
is a tiny plantation in the field—I mean the
Park—date 1874, connected with the garden
by a turf walk, with a breadth of flowers and
young evergreen trees intermixed, on either
hand. Here all my most favourite flowers
grow in wild profusion. The turf walk is
lost, after a break of Golden Yew, in a little
wood—a few paces round—just large enough

for the birds to build in, and with room for
half-a-dozen wild Hyacinths and a dozen
Primroses under the trees; with moss, Wood
Sorrel, and white and puce-coloured Periwinkles, and many a wild thing, meant to
encourage the delusion of a savage wild ! I
am afraid I never can be quite serious about
a garden; I always am inclined to find
delight in fancies, and reminiscences of a
child's garden, and the desire to get everything into it if I could. This "Fantaisie"
was a dream of delight during the past
summer—from April, when a nightingale
possessed in song the half-hidden entrance
under low embowering Elm branches and
Syringa—through all the fairy days and
months, up to quite lately. Yes, even last
week, it was fragrant with Mignonette and
Ragged Jack (I mean that Alpine Pink
Dianthus Plumarius), gay with yellow Zinnias and blue Salvia in rich luxuriance, with
a host of smaller, less showy things—with
bunches of crimson Roses, and pink La
France, blooming out from a perfect mist
of white and pinkish Japan Anemones, white
Sweet Peas, and a few broad Sunflowers

towering at the back—their great stems coruscating all over with stars of gold; and here and there clusters of purple Clematis, leaning sadly down from a faggot of brown leaves and dead, wiry stalks,—or turning from their weak embrace of some red-brown Cryptomeria Elegans. Even last week the borders throughout the garden looked filled and cheerful—brilliant with scarlet Lobelia and tall deep red Phloxes, and bushes of blue-leaved starry Marguerites, and the three varieties of Japan Anemone, with strange orange Tigridias and Auratum Lilies and Ladies' Pincushion (*Scabious*, the "Saudades" of the Portuguese language of Flowers), and every kind of late as well as summer Roses, the evening Primrose (*Œnothera*) making sunshine in each shady spot, with here and there the burning flame of a Tritoma; though these last have not done well this autumn.

Out near the carriage drive are Golden Rod and crimsoned patches of Azalea, and a second blow of late and self-sown Himalayan (so called) Poppies. In one narrow bit of south border one finds that pretty blue daisy (*Kaulfussia Amelloides*)—such an odd, pretty little thing. I remember a bed of it in the garden of my childhood, and I possess a portrait of it, done for me by my mother; and then, never met with it again till a year or two ago, when unexpectedly it looked up at me, somewhere in a remote country churchyard. I am afraid our present stock comes from that very plant. Until now, the long border of many-coloured Verbenas was still rather gay, and the three east gables of the house were all aflame with Virginian Creeper. But two days of rain spoilt us entirely. The variegated Maple slipped its white garment all at once in the night, causing a melancholy gap. In the kitchen garden a bright red Rose or two remains, but along the east border the half-blown buds are rotted away. In the centre of one drenched pink bloom I saw a poor drone, drowned as he sat idly there. Small black-headed titmice are jerking about among the tallest Rose trees, insect hunting; and still tinier wrens flit here and there, bent on the same quest. Great spotted missel thrushes are now haunting the pillar Yews, beginning

to taste the luscious banquet just ready for
them. While thus perched amongst the
sweet scarlet Yew berries and dark foliage,
the thrushes always bring to one's mind a
design in old tapestry.

And this reminds me of the good and
abundant fruit-feast we have ourselves enjoyed this season. Strawberries and Rasp-
berries were not much, but such Gooseberries,
Apricots, and Nectarines! Peaches, plenty
enough, but no flavour. Figs, enough
to satisfy even *our* greediness,—though we
have but one tree, on a west wall. Pears,
especially Louise Bonne, first-rate and
plenty. Apples, a small crop, but sufficient.
Wood Strawberries have been ripening under
the windows till within the last few days: I
planted them there for the sake of the
delicious smell of the leaves when decaying
—a smell said to be perceptible only to the
happy few. Nuts (Filberts and Kentish
Cobs) were plentiful, but we were only
allowed a very few dishes of them. A large
number of nuthatches settled in the garden
as soon as the nuts were ripe ; they nipped
them off, and, carrying them to the old

Acacia tree, which stands conveniently near, stuck them in the rough bark and cracked them at their ease (or rather punched holes in them). The Acacia's trunk at one time quite bristled over with the empty nut-shells, while the husks lay at the roots. The fun of watching these busy thieves at work more than made up for the loss of nuts. We had a great abundance of large green and yellow wall Plums, also a fair quantity of purple. Of sweet Cherries, unless gathered rather unripe, my dear blackbirds and starlings never leave us many. But there were a good lot of Morellos; they don't care a bit for them. Whilst on the subject of fruit, let me say that never a shot is fired in the garden, unless to destroy weazels. Our "garden's sacred round" is free to every bird that flies—the delight of seeing them, and of hearing their music, compensates to the full any ravages they may indulge in. Thanks to netting without stint, and our Gardener's incomparable patience and longsuffering, I enjoy the garden and my birds in peace; and if they ever do any harm, we never know it; fruit and green

Peas never fail us! .. Here is a sunny
morning; and the cows are whisking their
tails under the Elms, as if it were July.
But indeed the last lingering trace of summer has vanished: the garden is in ruins,
and already the redbreast is singing songs
of triumph.

NOVEMBER.

2

"The True Pleasure of a Garden."—BACON.

II.

NOVEMBER, 1882.

Of Blossoms, Buds, and Bowers—Of May and June
and July Flowers.

November 3.—The ruin is complete! and
cleared away, too. . . . Yet there is consolation, and something very comfortable, in the
neatness of the dug borders, and the beds
made up for the winter.

The symmetrically banked-up Celery—
crested with the richest green, in the
kitchen garden—rather takes my fancy; so
also does the fine bit of colour in some huge
heaps of dead leaves, that I see already
stored in the rubbish yard. The dead
leaves have to be swept away from lawn and
garden walks—but I believe we do not con-

sider any except those of Beach and Oak to
be of much service. It is my heresy, that
leaves do not fall till the goodness of them
has decayed. They are of use, however, when
left to cover the ground above tender roots.
In the Fantaisie the earthy bed can scarce
be seen, so close lies this warm counterpane
of leaves! The great Elms, on the greyest
days, now make sunshine of their own.
Their lofty breadths of yellow gold tower
above the zone of garden trees. When the
sun illumines them, and the light winds pass,
it is a dream to watch the glittering fall of
autumn leaves. The ancient times return,
and Jove once more showers gold around
some sleeping Danae! During the first days
of the month, the parterr was done, Tulips
put in, and a lot of Crocuses in double row.
In a few beds the dwarf evergreens, which
had been removed for the summer, are
planted in again—just to make the parterr's
emptiness look less cheerless from the
dining-room windows. Between these small
evergreen bushes, in their season, will come
up spikes of Hyacinths, of varied hue. I
do not care for a whole bed of Hyacinths

or Tulips; they give me little real pleasure
unless the colours be mixed. One chief
charm of a garden, I think, depends on
surprise. There is a kind of dulness in
Tulips and Hyacinths, sorted, and coming
up all one size and colour. I love to watch
the close-folded Tulip bud, rising higher
and higher daily—almost hourly—from its
brown bed; and never to be quite certain
of the colour that is to be, till one morning
I find the rose, or golden, or ruby cup in
all its finished beauty; perhaps not at all
what was expected   And then, amid these
splendours, will suddenly appear one shorter
or taller than he rest, of the purest, rarest
white. How that white Tulip, coming as it
were by chance, is valued ! And so, again
this year a mixed lot are planted. There
was a time when we had only one Tulip in
all the garden. I used to look for it regu-
larly in a certain shady border under a
Laburnum tree; an old-fashioned, dull,
purple and white-striped flower, but it never
failed to show, at the very end of every
season. I had a regard for that Tulip, and
last summer it was a disappointment vainly

to wait for its appearance in the accustomed
spot.   Many there were of its kind, surpassing it in loveliness; but then they were not
the same.

Hyacinth beds will be a new thing here,
but I doubt if they will make us quite
so happy as has hitherto the unexpected
advent of some stray pyramid of small
odorous bells, pink, blue, or creamy-white,
in out-of-the-way places about the garden.
After their flowering is over, the pot-bulbs
are always turned out somewhere in the
borders.   When a plant has lived with us
for a time under the same roof, or even in
the green-house, giving out for us its whole
self of sweetness or of beauty, it seems so
cruel that it should at last be thrown away
as if worthless and forgotten!   Some Narcissus that have had their day have just
been put into a round bed on the further
lawn, mixed with the " Mrs. Sinkins " white
Pink; and there is a rim all round of double
lilac Primroses.   I have long wished to have
plenty of that dear old neglected Primrose;
so now we have a number of healthy roots
from an old garden in Derbyshire.   In the

centre of this bed is a very tall dead Cupressus, one of our few failures in transplantation last spring. A Cobæa, which was to have grown up quick and made a "bonnie green gown" for the poor bare tree, proved failure number two. It absolutely refused to grow, or do anything but look stunted and miserable, till one day, late in October, there it was running up the tree as fast as possible, clothing every twig with leaves and tendrils, and large, deep, bell-like blossoms! Its day must be short, however, at the wrong end of the year, and even now its bells are chilled to a greenish hue. A fine red climbing Rose on one side, and one of the old Blairii on the other, will make a kinder and more beautiful summer garment.

We have made a new Lavender border, and now I hope to have enough for the bees, and afterwards enough, when dried, to lay within the drawers and wardrobes, and give us "all the perfume of summer, when summer is gone;" enough, too, for potpourri, though we do not always make this fresh each year. It takes time, and there is so little time in these days! and often the

Roses are too wet, and the Lavender too
scarce. The recipe we use is an old one:
the paper is yellow, and the ink faded. But
our best pot-pourri of these days comes not
near the undying fragance of some Rose
leaves—three generations old—that we still
preserve in one or two old covered jars
and bowls of Oriental porcelain. Along the
south wall, an oblong bed is planted with
dark purple Heartsease, and two more with
yellow. There are six beds, and in the
spring they will glow resplendently with
a setting of Crocuses, white, yellow, and
lilac; meanwhile a good layer of cocoa-
nut fibre gives a look of comfort for the
winter; and moreover, rather annoys the
field-mice.

Under the Holly hedge, facing south, a
narrow border has been made ready to
receive a quantity of white Iris roots. The
Holly hedge, planted for shelter and for
pleasure, along a broad walk on one side of
the carriage drive, is not in itself a success
as yet. It was put in four years ago, but
the trees were too old, I think; this year it
is flushed all over with scarlet berries.

I am sorry to have to remove my beloved white Irises, but they have increased so enormously as to make some change necessary. Nearly twenty years ago I carried home from the south of France a few small roots in a green pitcher. For half that time they grew and multiplied on the sunny terraces of a sweet Somersetshire garden, and now for ten other years the same roots, transplanted here, have flourished, if possible, still more abundantly. It may be fancy only, but I think our white Irises might not have succeeded as they do, had they not been loved so well. Everybody has a favourite flower, I suppose— the white Iris is mine—the Fleur-de-lys of France—the lily of Florence. Nothing can be more refined and lovely than the thin, translucent petals. To see these flowers at their best, one must get up and go into the garden at five o'clock on some fine morning at the end of May. I did it once, and as I walked beside their shining rows in the clear daylight, I felt there were no such pearly shadows, nor any such strange purity in the whiteness of other flowers. We have given away a great many, but I fear I am not altogether sorry that they do not seem always to succeed elsewhere as they do with us. I am trying to collect every different Iris I know of. We have now several which are very beautiful, and we should have more were it not that numbers die off after, perhaps, one short summer's loveliness. They dwindle and become sickly, and then altogether disappear. Almost our whole stock of one well-established kind—an old inhabitant of the garden—was destroyed by mice two seasons ago. The flower is bronze-brown, with a golden blaze in the middle. La Marquise (Iris Lurida?), an old-fashioned dove-coloured sort, with purple frays on the falls, will grow anywhere. So will the large, broad-leaved, pale lilac kind, and the yellow Algerian. A little black wild Iris, that fringes the vineyard trenches about Florence, we have either lost or it will not flower. They call it here "La Vedova." I brought home some roots once from Bellosguardo, and we put them in where all the warmest rays of the south sun would find them. But only the long, narrow,

wild onion-like leaves appear—or, I fancy,
they are the Vedova's leaves. Still I do not
lose hope, but watch for it always when
March comes round; and some day, somewhere, I think, my little "widow" is sure
to surprise me The wild yellow Italian
Tulip, that came with the Iris, succeeds here
well. The patch of pale gold never fails, by
the first week in April, to enliven the sunny
side of a Yew hedge. A few untidy yellow
blooms, supported on slender limp stalks,
live there, just the same as in their own
dear Italy. I stoop down to gather one, and
for a moment the English garden is not
there. . . . Before me lies a grassy vineyard
path—there are the great open farm-sheds,
full of sunlight and sunlit shade—and the
pair of grey long-horned oxen, calmly
waiting for the yoke. Near them, with her
knitting, stands a patient sad-eyed woman,
while happy children run down the path at
play, or tie up bunches of yellow Tulips
under the fig-trees. . . . Then there is a tall,
white flag Iris, whose place is not yet fairly
fixed. It is a handsome thing, and quite
unlike the Fleur-de-lys. I think of mixing

it in with the yellow Flags and Osmunda
Regalis beside the little watercourse.   Last
July, to watch the slow blooming of some
Japanese Iris in the kitchen garden gave
me intense delight.   They grew tall and
straight, with curiously ribbed leaves.   The
single flower at the top of each stem opened
out very flat, with rounded petals, rich
purple in colour, and measuring nearly
seven inches across.   One saw at once it
was the purple flower the Prince, in the
German fairy tale, found on the mountains,
and carried off to disenchant his love with,
in the old witch's cottage by the wood—only
a large pearl lay in the centre of that flower.
(There is no such thing as anachronism in
fairy tales!)

We have gathered in our harvest of winter decorations for the hall and corridors.
There is Pampas-grass with its silken plumes,
and soft tassels of all kinds of downy German
grasses, and Everlastings of all lovely shades
of orange and red.   They have hung in
bunches head downwards in the vinery to
dry for weeks past, and they will last for
the next twelve months as fresh as they are

now. I have been told of a great bouquet
of Everlasting Flowers, in a Dutch gentle-
man's drawing-room at the Cape, which was
affirmed to be two hundred years old. We
have sheaves of Honesty, also—" Money in
your Pocket," as the poor say—which are
to gleam like flakes of mother-o'-pearl in
the firelight of December's dusky afternoons.
We left plenty in the garden, however,
where they will stand a good deal more of
rough weather before they fall to pieces.
Honesty is always handsome, in all stages of
its growth ; and like the people who take
things easily, it thrives everywhere. With
us it is quite at home in a damp north
border, close under a line of Elms. All
through June and July, the violet glow of
a mass of it in full bloom made a brilliant
effect ; and now, in these November days,
the ripe seed-vessels are transformed—their
outer husk has shelled off, leaving only the
silvery centre. The other day, in my early
walk, just where the Allée Verte ends (no
longer green, it is now a golden corridor,
with, underfoot, crisp russet leaves), I seemed
to come upon—not Wordsworth's host of

dancing Daffodils, but a company of spirits !
The slanting sunbeams fell upon a clump of
Honesty, and touched with fire every one of
the myriad little silver moons. Though no
wind stirred, they seemed to quiver with
ghostly life in a shimmer of opal lights.

Nov. 18.—Winter is striding on, and every
bit of colour in the garden becomes more
precious than ever. Only a few days ago
I made a nosegay of crimson summer Roses,
a fine Auratum Lily, a Gladiolus, a Welsh
Poppy, and a large red-rimmed annual
Poppy, with a wonderful spray of Flexuosa
Honeysuckle, that filled the room with its
fragrance. A little while since, in one
sheltered corner, Salvia Patens still held
its own in unsullied blue. Marigolds were
plenty ; St. John's Wort must have made
a mistake in its dates, for it was all over
polished yellow buds ready to unclose ;
Mignonette and a few Sweet Peas lingered
still. Here and there one came upon a
white Snap-dragon or a flash of rose-red
Phlox ("Farewell Summers" they call them
in the West). It was impossible not to

admire the vigour and beauty of Primroses
and Polyanthus of every colour. One only
hopes this abundant autumnal bloom may
not interfere with their blossoming in the
sprin ; it is certainly finer than I ever
remember in former seasons. A rockwork
of big flints was quite gay with Virginian
Stock and Primroses. To-day the frost is
most severe. The Marigolds look unlike
themselves, with a white cap border of
frost, quilled round their orange faces ; the
half-opened buds in a Tea Rose bed are like
fancy Moss Roses ; only the moss is white,
and every leaf is fringed with little sharp-
pointed crystals. The China Rose tree by
the green door in the wall is covered with
pink roses, which I forgot to gather yesterday
for my flower-glasses. This morning the
frost has curiously changed them. The
delicate petals are stiffened all through, as if
they were turned into wax models, though
their lovely pink is not dimned, and they
smell as sweet as if nothing had happened.
By this time our Irish Yews have resumed
their wonted sadness. The berries are all
carried off, and the blackbirds have fattened

so well on them, and on the bunches of grapes
(left for their benefit on the house Vines),
that they rise from the lawn quite heavily. I
never saw such fat blackbirds! The seed of
the Yew berries, which is believed to be the
only poisonous part, is, I think, in most
cases, left unswallowed; and in one little
tree I found the remnants of an old nest filled
with a compact mass of Yew seeds. The
large blue titmouse carries off his berry to
the Sumach tree, and there pecks off the
pulp, holding it down with his foot. The
larger thrushes are gone, I know not where;
only one small bird, with richly spotted
breast, is still seen about the grass, under
the Stone Pine.

The Chrysanthemums in the greenhouse
must have the last word. Nothing could be
more beautiful than they are now, and have
been for several weeks past. Some of the
Japanese kinds are indescribably lovely;
arrayed in tints that make one think of a
sea-shell, or the clouds about an April sunrise. There is something, perhaps, in their
delicious confusion of petals, that helps this
wonderful effect of colour. The other sorts,

which are stiffer in arrangement, and more
decided in colour, are to me somewhat
less delightful. A tiny wren was among
the Chrysanthemums this morning, noise-
lessly flitting in and out, like a little shade;
evidently in a state of the highest enjoyment.
No doubt I and the bird both took our
pleasure with them—in different ways!

DECEMBER.

"Once a Dream did Weave a Shade." ..

"He who goeth into his garden to look for spiders and cob-
webs will doubtless find them; but he who goes out to seek a
flower may return to his house with one blooming in his bosom."

III.

DECEMBER.

Of Spiders' Webs, Christmas Roses, King Arthur,
and the Tree I Love.

December 6.—Among the strange and beautiful sights of the garden during the hard
hoar-frost that ushered in the first days of
the month, not the least beautiful were
the spiders' webs. Passing along the Larch
Walk, the oak palings that divide us on that
side from the new road (the old road, made
by Richard, King of the Romans, in the thir-
teenth century, is now within the grounds)
were hung all over with white rags—or so it
seemed at first sight. And then, just for one
second, that curious momentary likeness of
like to unlike chanced. I remembered the
street of palaces at Genoa, the day when I saw

it last; the grand old walls covered with
fluttering rags of advertisements—yes, advertisements in English: "Singer's Sewing
Machine." The white rags on our palings
were spiders' webs both new and old, a
marvellous number, thus crystallized, as it
were, into existence by the frost, where
scarcely one had been before. In open
weather the webs are as good as invisible to
human eyes; but now that frost had thickened
the minutest threads to the size of Berlin
wool—though in beauty of texture they
resembled fine white velvet chenille—there
was a sudden revelation of these wonderful
works of art! One feels, if the nets show
only half as large and thick to a fly's eye,
the spider's trade must be a poor one. Here
is a calculation that will probably interest
nobody: 567 feet of pales over 5 feet high,
and an average of 18 webs to every 9 feet.
It may prove, however, something of the un-
suspected multitude of spiders in a given
area, though it is nothing to the acres of
ploughed land that the level sun-ray of an
autumn afternoon will show completely
netted over with gossamer. Making the

most of a few minutes' inspection—for I
should myself have frozen had I watched
much longer these frozen webs—I could
see but two varieties of work—the cobweb
which usurped the corners, and the beautiful wheel-within-wheel net. In them all
one might observe once more that ever-
recurring stern immutability of the thing
called Instinct. Here, for instance, are two
sets of spiders living close neighbours for
years together. Each set makes its snares on
an opposite plan; and although they cannot
help seeing each other's work continually,
neither takes the least hint from the other.
The plain cobweb is never made more intri-
cate; the artist of the wheel never dreams
that she might do her spinning to a simpler
pattern. Happy people! They trouble not
their heads about improvements; yet, on
looking closer at the last-named webs, there
seemed something of the faintest indication
of a slight individuality; so far at least, that
in a dozen nets there would be five or six
worked within a square of four lines, while
the remainder had five, tied rather carelessly
in a knot below. Perhaps the variation

marks two distinct species; or it may be only accidental. Next day every visible trace of the strong beautiful webwork I had so admired was gone with the frost. The spider may have "spread her net abroad with cords" as usual, but there was no magician's wand to touch it.

The orchard ought to be very gay in the spring. Daffodils have been dropped in all over the turf, and a round patch dug round each Apple tree is to be filled with yellow Wallflowers. This is an experiment, and I do not feel sure that I shall like the flowers so well as the trees simply growing out of the grass. A change, however, is always pleasant; though, perhaps, one might hardly care to lay out the garden differently every year, as the Chinese are said to do. I had a dream, of the orchard grass enamelled with many-coloured Crocuses—in loving reminiscence of certain flowery Olive grounds I know; but after all, the imitation would have been as poor as a winter sky compared to the glowing blue of June. I am not without hope some day—that golden "some day" which so seldom comes—to naturalize in our orchards the real *enamelling* of the Olive groves—that often-used phrase is too hard in sound and in its usual meaning to express the loveliness of those lilac star Anemones— with here and there a salmon-pink, or a fiery scarlet, blazing like a sun in the living green beneath the trees. I used to think nothing on this earth could come so near a vision of the star-strewn fields of Paradise.

In the north, or entrance court, we have been busy transplanting some large Apple trees that had overgrown their place, and setting free the trimmed Yews between which they grew. The blackness of these formal, cut Yews shows well against the old walls, which are covered with very aged Green- gages and golden Drops. On the turf be- tween each of the pyramid Yews, broad ob- long beds have been made; in April we hope to plant them with pink China Roses, which are to grow very dwarf, and to flower the whole year through! The border round the Roses may be blue Nemophila; or perhaps the lovely Santolina Fragrans, with the soft grey foliage.

I think the "going in" to one's house
should be as bright and cheerful as it is
possible to make it. But how hard it is to
brighten up a north aspect! ours has hitherto been far too gloomy. In the garden,
the bed of Roman Roses is warmly matted
over for the winter. This brave little red
China Rose is one of my great favourites;
it goes on flowering for ever! Even now,
when the matting is raised a little bit, I can
see buds and leaves and the red of opening
blooms. I call it the Roman Rose chiefly
because it grows at Florence; which is so
very Irish, that I think there must have been
some better reason now forgotten. The Rose
hedges in the beautiful Boboli Gardens are
crimsoned over with blossoms as early as
the end of March; with us, however, it
needs protection when planted in the open
ground.

Under the east wall is our only Christmas
Rose; it is a very large plant, and over it
was built up, about a month ago, a little
green bower of Spruce Fir branches. The
shelter is to save the blooms from frost,
which so often tarnishes their whiteness

with red. Almost daily, as I passed, I have
peeped in to watch the cluster of white buds
nestled snugly within. The buds have duly
swelled and lifted one by one their heads,
and now this morning our first bunch of
perfect Christmas Roses has been gathered.
This flower must, I think, be dear to every
one with a heart for flowers. Its expression
is so full of innocence and freshness—for it is
not only human persons who have expression
in their faces! and then the charm of its
Myrtle-like stamens and clear-cut petals—
snow-cold to the touch—and its pretty way
of half-hiding among the dark leaves—
always ready to be found when sought—and
always with so many more blossoms than
had been hoped for! To some, indeed, the
associations bound up with the Christmas
Rose—with even the sound of its name—
may be dearer than all its outward loveliness;
recalling, perhaps, the house and garden of
their childhood, and happy Christmases of
long ago; "the old familiar faces," and tones
of the voices that are gone. I must here
make the confession that last year, in my
anxiety for the whitest possible of blossoms,

I had glass placed over the plant; and in spite of warnings, put matting over that; all which ended at Christmas in a fine show of green Roses! In the pits there are several of the smaller kind coming on in pots, which will soon be ready to cut. These are easy enough in their ways. But the Christmas Rose out in the border is a difficult thing to grow; full of quirks and fancies, and like a woman, hard to please. Once, however, it settles down in any spot, it will thrive there; and then will sooner die than take to a new place.

Dec. 13.—Our second white frost has vanished, and the grass appears again with a moist and pleasant smell. The forest of the Fantaisie is thinned, and the encircling Laurels trimmed. The whole took just half a winter's day to do. At the end of the turf walk, between the bushes and the golden Yews, peers out a Spindle tree, with its pink and scarlet fruit. The birds seem not to care for it, for the fruit is all there—untouched. I wonder if the name of Spindle comes from the unnatural thinness of the tree!

After these many years of working to a special end, we seem now to have almost reached it in one direction, for the garden looks well-nigh as green and furnished in winter as in summer—so far, at least, as the outline of verdure goes. The Yew hedges, and Pines, and perennial greens are at their best now, in mid-winter; they would even seem to have grown and thickened out since the summer died away. Watching the growth of these trees and hedges has been the delight and solace of many a troubled time, and one cannot but feel the most affectionate interest in them. In the centre of a triangular-shaped bit of lawn, surrounded by Conifers, we have placed a large stone vase on a square stone pedestal. The vase is old and grey, and had long stood in another place, where it made no show. The grey stone looks well against the warm greens that back it, and will look better when the season comes to fill it with bright summer flowers. The trees that stand around all wear a sort of charmed double life—at least to me—silently, fancifully.

It was at a time of sickness that the sleep-

less hours of the long winter nights came to
be passed in spirit with the trees in the garden, and especially with half-a-dozen or so
of our beautiful straight young Pines.   Dare
I tell the secret ?   They all became knights
and ladies of King Arthur's Court! The great
Wellingtonia standing a little apart is Arthur
himself. The Nordmanniana, with its whorls
of deepest green and strong upward shoot of
fifteen inches in the year, is Sir Launcelot.
The gold-green softly-feathered Douglas Fir,
Sir Bedevere. The young Cedar of Lebanon,
with fretted boughs of graceful downward
sweep, Sir Agravaine.   Sir Bors is a
rounded solemn English Yew, of slow and
steadfast growth.   Sir Palomides—a fine
pillar-shaped Thuia—towers between Sir
Gawaine and Sir Gaheris, who are both clad
in the wondrous green with almost metallic
lustre of Cupressus Lawsoniana erecta viridis.
These all stand round the triangular lawn,
and amongst them comes, by some strange
chance, St. Eulalie, a lovely Pine (*Abies
Amabilis*), whose robe of grey-blue tufted
foliage wraps her feet, and trails upon the
grass.

Beyond, on the long lawn next "the park," stands Sir Tristram, the fine young Pinsapo ; he all but perished in the frost of 1879-80, but now he seems to have drawn new strength and vigorous green from that nearly fatal conflict with his terrible enemy. On the house lawn, the Deodara, is the fairy Morgan-le-faye. Near her stood Sir La Cote-mal-taille, an ill-formed Lawsoniana ; but he is now transplanted elsewhere. King Mark is a rather wretched ill-grown Cedrus, in summer almost hidden by Laburnums. Dame Bragwaine is a curious Cryptomeria Elegans ; she has so many names (seven, at least, that I know of), and she takes such odd diverse disguises ! once, loaded with heavy snow, she had to be supported by a stake, and took the semblance of a bear leaning on a ragged staff. In summer she is green, and in winter she wears a dress of purple brown ; in rain or heavy dew she is spangled all over with diamonds and pearls. Queen Guinevere was never represented ; no tree was found to fit her character. But near King Arthur and Sir Tristram, the two great Pampas tufts, still waving wintry plumes, are "La Beale Isoude" and "Isoude les Blaunch Mains."

From our foolish garden-dreaming let us rest, and turn with a long look of revering love to the great Oak, that stands in his strength out in the park field, beyond the garden. On three sides round are lines of guardian Elms, in all their pride of delicate leafless intricacy; alone, amid the leafless ones, rises the Oak, wearing still his crown of brown, sere leaves. Smooth and straight grows up the giant stem, full twenty feet to the spring of the lowest branch. Two brother Oaks stand on either side. Their form is more rounded, more perfect; but high above them the great Oak uprears his head— unconcerned, and grandly branched, though shattered by every fierce west wind that blows. Every storm works some loss, but from the way each torn limb lies, you would say he had thrown it down in proud defiance. The wood-pigeons shelter among the summer leaves; the autumn ripens a rich store of acorns; and now, as I survey him from the terrace walk, or gaze upwards from the wet dead leaves beneath, through all the mystery

of his bare and spreading boughs, I think
of Keats' stanza—

> " In a drear-nighted December,
>   Too happy, happy tree,
>   Thy branches ne'er remember
>   Their green felicity ;
>   The North cannot undo them,
>   With a sleety whistle through them,
>   Nor frozen thawings glue them
>   From budding at the prime."

The Oak is to my mind the tree of trees ;
and the destruction of its foliage, by insect
ravages, that has year by year saddened so
many parks and woods, has not come near us,
I rejoice to say. Our few (there are but four or
five) are safe as yet. I heard the gardener of
one great place that had suffered much ac-
knowledge as the cause the scarcity of birds.

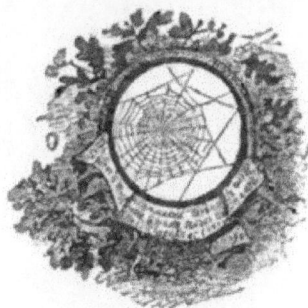

4

JANUARY, 1883.

"To the Attentive Eye, each Moment of the Year has its own Beauty."—EMERSON.

IV.

JANUARY.

Of Field-Mice, and the Thorn of Joseph of Arimathea—
Of "Poor Johnnys"—A Lilac Gem—and Greenhouse Flowers.

January 5, 1883.—A large body of the army
of the small ones of the earth has attacked
us, and it is no fault of theirs if we are not
despoiled of the best of our spring delights.
The field-mice have at length found out the
Crocuses; we, on our side, have set traps
in their way, and large numbers have fallen
—quite flat, poor little things!—under the
heavy bricks. We believe we should have
slain many more, had not some clever creature made a practice of examining the traps
during the night, devouring the cheese, and

in some way withdrawing the bit of stick, so as to let the brick fall harmless. Suspicion points towards one person especially—the old white fox-terrier, who lives in the stables, and is master (in his own opinion) of all that department, and whom neither gates nor bars can prevent going anywhere he chooses to go. "Impossible!" says he, with Mirabeau; "don't mention that stupid word!" Up to this time field-mice have not troubled us much. In the days when there was always a hawk or two hovering over the ploughed land, or keeping watch over the green meadows, and when we used to hear the owls in the summer nights, and saw the white owl who lived somewhere near by sail silently in the grey of evening across the lawn—in those days we knew little of the plague of field-mice. But now we have changed all that; cheap gun licences have put a gun into every one's hand, the vermin is ruthlessly shot, and the balance of Nature is destroyed.

It is rather a fearful pleasure that we take just now to mark the unwonted earliness of green things of all kinds. One cannot help

dreading that some great check will happen
later on in the year; and yet it may be an
omen for good that the birds' full concert
has only just begun, in these dark mornings,
amongst the trees of the garden. The saying goes in Scotland, "If the birds pipe
afore Christmas they'll greet after;" and
so far as I know, not a note was sung till
December 30. The birds served our Hollies
a good turn at Christmas. In November
the Hollies were scarlet with berries, and
one thought with a shudder of how they
would have to suffer, when the time came
for Christmas decorations; then occurred
two short severe frosts, and, to my joy,
the Holly trees were swept clear of every
tempting spot of scarlet before Christmas,
and thus were saved the customary reck-
less breaking and tearing of branches.
Dear birds! Does any one ever think, I
wonder, sitting in the summer shade near
"some moist, bird-haunted English lawn,"
how dull it would be without them—how
much they enhance for us the grace and
charm of the garden and the country? It
is their gay light-heartedness that is so

delightful, and that we should miss so much if they were not there. Who ever saw a grave bird ?—at least I mean a grave little one—the bigger the sadder it is, with them. Their very labours of nest-building, and of feeding their young ones, are done like a merry bit of child's play! The birds' never-failing interest in life is like a sort of tonic to those who love them. Michelet felt this when he called them "des êtres innocents, dont le mouvement, les voix, et les jeux, sont comme le sourire de la Création."

I do not remember having seen before in mid-winter a Hawthorn hedge bursting out into leaf! At the end of last month, however, there were strong young shoots and fully formed leaves on some of the Quicks in a hedge planted last spring in our lane. I have known nothing like this, except the Glastonbury Thorn. There is one of these strange Thorns, a large tree, growing just within the park gates of Marston Bigot, in Somersetshire. It used to bloom with great regularity in mild winters about this time. Tufts of flowers came all over the branches, smelling as sweet as Hawthorn in May. I

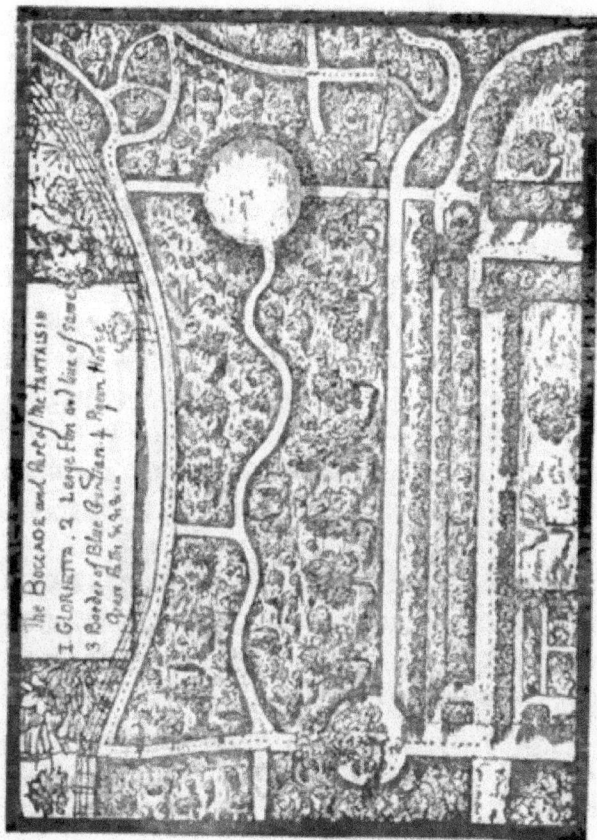

The BOCCAGE and Rest of the FRUTALISH
1 GLORIETTA. 2 Large Elm and Vine of stone
3 Border of Blew Gradian & Pigon Houses
green Elms & &c...

have often cut a long spray all wreathed with
pearly bloom, on New Year's Eve, in former
years. The flowers come with scarce a sign
of leaf about them, and they are rather
smaller than those of the common May.
The emerald green of turf, thickly sprinkled
with Daisies, seems also an unusual sight
for January. The first green glow on the
grass and the first Daisy we are surely used
to hail as signs of approaching spring. On
the lawn, too, a yellow Buttercup, careless
of the heavy roller, has dared to hold up its
head !

Jan. 8.—The weather has been for many
weeks so dark and gloomy, that the rare sunshine which shone upon the land to-day was
as welcome and nearly as unlooked for as
May flowers in January. The house stood
blocked out in sun and shadow. Magnolia
Grandiflora, which covers the south-east
gable, looked grand in this flood of radiance.
Standing before it, the refrain of a wild
canzonetta I once heard, chanted forth lazily
in the little sun-steeped piazza of an old
Italian town, came back to the mind's ear—
" Oh, splendid bella ! " The eye, soon tired,

however, of so much dazzling brilliance in the polished foliage, each leaf reflecting back the sun, follows the ascending lines of beauty up above the pointed roofs, where the soft golden rust of the topmost leaves' inner lining meets the deep blue, cloudless sky. Next the Magnolia, just under the painting-room window, is a Flexuosa Honeysuckle which has not lost a leaf this winter. New shoots and twists of brightest green, set with young leaves two and two, are springing all over it. One tender shoot, indeed, has had the heart to curl twice round a branch, sending out a length of spray beyond.

Hard by the Flexuosa flourished once a fine Gum Cistus. To my sorrow, it perished in the frost of two winters back. The aroma of its gummy foliage, under the noontide sun, would penetrate deliciously through the open windows. We lost that winter all but one of our Gum Cistus, and their destruction was so universal that there was a difficulty in replacing them. I like the Gum Cistus best when growing upon the lawn. The snow of fallen petals on the grass seems right, and gives no sense of untidiness, there.

The loss of the Cistus, however, made room
for better growth to the old Maiden's-blush
Rose in the corner, by another window.
She has hard work, anyhow, to hold her
own against the flowery smothering of an
Everlasting Pea, which persists in spreading beyond all bounds, notwithstanding the
hints it yearly receives from knife and spade.
Further on, still under the south front, a
white Hepatica (Poor Johnny) is already
shyly blooming. The root is sheltered by
its own undecayed leaves; other plants of
the same kind being quite bare. Hepaticas
in England almost always look discontented,
and this is no marvel to any who have
seen them wild in their own place. I remember as clear as yesterday the oy of
finding the blue Hepatica for the first time.
It was in a narrow lovely valley at Men-
tone, on a mossy bank beside the little
stony river. We were gathering Violets,
which abound in that place; but on the
edge of the bank, and over its steep side,
intermingled with deep Moss and Ferns,
there was another blue, which was not the
blue of Violets. It was like the surprise

and wonder of a new world thus unawares
to come upon such a flower—the beloved of
childhood—in such rich profusion—a flower
we had never seen before that happy day,
save in rare scanty patches, in some damp
garden border! About the same time I saw
also both the pink and white Hepaticas,
from the Pine woods on the slopes of the
Alpes Maritimes. In a corner near the
Hepaticas is a little patch of Violets with
Bella Donna Lilies. The Lilies are sending
up strong, healthy leaves, and that is about
all they will ever do to please me. Fine,
good roots were put in six years ago in this
choice south corner, where I believed they
could not but do well. But no; it is in
vain I watch and hope!—not one of those
exquisite "harmonies in ink" I so long to enjoy do they vouchsafe to give me. Possibly
they may object to the society of the Violets!

Primroses have been with us more or less
since September last, and now they are more
abundant than ever—all colours—red, brown,
yellow, white, sulphur: the garden is quite
full of Primroses. Roses, also, we have
scarcely been without all winter. Within

the walled garden there are real red Rosebuds, rather tightly closed up, but capable
of opening any day. Many Rose-bushes
have never lost their old leaves, and some
are already putting forth new. On the top
of the wall I perceived to-day a white spot
—it was a Gloire de Dijon—looking very
pale, but fully opened ; and below it the
Marcartney and an Apricot Tea Rose are in
bud. A space of kitchen garden wall by the
north iron gate is resplendent with Jasminum
Nudiflorum, and close by, the bare branches
of a Fig tree are already pointed with green,
recalling in a dim way the Fig trees of the
South, which in March glow like great
branched candlesticks lighted up with flames
of golden-green, in honour of the coming
festa of spring. The Pyrus Japonica—a
very old plant—has opened two coral cups.
But the gem of the whole garden just now
is a small, most delicately yet brilliantly
tinted lilac Iris.* The contrast between it
and the rich dark green of its reed-like
leaves, amidst which the flower shines, is
charming. It is only in the mildest of winters

* *Iris Ensata.*

that it ventures to appear. Last year the
date of its blooming first was February 10.
There are several tufts of foliage, but as
yet only this one perfect flower, and we find
rarely more than half-a-dozen in the season.
In "the land of flowers," however, which
I believe to be its own, the paths of many
a Cypress and Ilex-shaded garden must be
lined with lilac and green, at this very time.
I often think how little use is made of that
most poetical of colours, lilac—"lalock," as
our grandmothers used to pronounce it. It
was Schiller's favourite colour; but I hardly
know of any one else particularly caring for
it. Perhaps one reason may be, because it is
so hard to mix the most lovely shades of lilac
in painting, or in manufactured stuffs; and
then it is so evanescent. Even Nature
herself does not make use of lilac so freely
as of other colours—yellow being, I almost
think, her favourite. She has, however, hit
the mark indeed in the colouring of my lilac
gem; there is a sharpness in the flavour
—so to speak—which makes it perfect. The
dear little winter Aconite—each bud of pure
clean yellow surrounded with its green frill

of leaves—appears here and there among
the damp dead leaves. Snowdrops are
showing daily whiter and larger above the
ground, and all sorts of green peaceful
spears are piercing in their strength, up
through the black mould everywhere.

We have got through some rather im-
portant work within the past three weeks.
A new Beech hedge has been planted on
the open side of a green walk or close,
already hedged in on one side. I once read
somewhere of how it is reckoned good for
the health to walk between Beech hedges,
the air being purified and freshened by
passing through the leaves. An old border,
full of bulbs and Damask Roses, has been
dug and rearranged. The Roses, which are
old plants, will be refreshed and improved
by the moving, and we shall add some day
one or two York and Lancaster Roses. In
this border the Grape Hyacinths have increased so rapidly that it is literally full of
them, and we are planting them about in
different places, some under the Deodara
(Morgan-le-faye) on the lawn, with Snowdrops and Daffodils. The Deodara is in the

wrong place, and was spreading so much as
to injure the effect of the Yew hedges. So,
instead of cutting it down, it is trimmed up
to eight feet or so from the grass; and for
this act I have had to brave a perfect storm
of adverse criticism! In a few months I
hope the stem will be clothed with Virginia
Creeper, which, when touched by Autumn's
fiery finger, will become a pillar of flame,
while wreaths of white Clematis (Virgin's
Bower) are to light up the green in summer.
Then we have been planting out four fine
tree Pæonies on the turf by the entrance
drive. In their season they will be as
beautiful as great cabbage roses.

There have been two days of frost and
bitter cold, and yet the impatient flowers are
not discouraged. At the further end of the
broad walk, down among the broken Fern
and withered leaves, a sense of colour is felt
in the border as one passes by. Ompha-
lodes'Verna (would that dear English names
were possible!)* is wide awake, and little

* Since writing this, I learn that the English name
is French Forget-me-not, and that it is a flower once
beloved of Queen Marie Antoinette.

eyes of cœrulean blue are looking upwards.
The Rock Roses are full of bud, and small
variegated-leaved Periwinkles, on a low wall,
already begin to tip their hanging sprays
with stars of misty grey. But the strangest
effort of all is a Foxglove spire of buds,
rising well up from its leaf-crowned root
on an ancient stump of Wistaria.

The mention of all these flowers would
make it seem, I fear, as if our garden were
even now a sort of flowery Paradise. The
truth is a sad contrast to every such idea ;
for though the beautiful things are all
in truth here, it would be difficult to de-
scribe the heavy gloom and damp of the
whole place. And so one turns more often
than usual to the greenhouse for consolation.
Small as ours is—only about fifteen paces
long—it is large enough for as much pleasure
as I desire, under glass. To me the open
garden is daily bread, the greenhouse "the
honey that crowns the repast." There
happens at this time to be a chord of colour
there, worth noting—ivory whiteness of
Roman Hyacinths, green of all exquisite
gradations, pale yellow of Meg Merrilies

Chrysanthemums ; others of a warmer yellow,
and pure white ; fairest pink of Primulas, and
a deep purple note, struck once or twice, of
Pleroma. What a flower that is! how
charming in its way of blooming sideways
on its stalk, to let the sun shine through
its violet translucence!

FEBRUARY.

With the Trees of the Garden.

V.

FEBRUARY.

Land of Mandragora and the Serpent Flower.

"There never was a juster debt
  Than what the dry do pay for wet;
  Never a debt was paid more nigh
  As what the wet do pay for dry!"

February 13.—If the West Country farmer's
rhyme prove true this year, the "dry" will
have a heavy debt to pay! Some of the
gravel walks in the garden are quite green,
along the sides where the almost ceaseless
rain flows down. All our dressed stone—
sun-dial, vases, steps—is discoloured and
green, and will all have to be scrubbed
with hot water and soap, like the rocks in

the great rockery once described in the
Gardener's Chronicle (vol. xviii., p. 747). A
large part of the grounds has been under
water nearly all through the winter; the
"wet," however, in which they sometimes
stand ankle deep for weeks, seems not to
do any harm to the evergreens here; whilst
we get from the floods charming landscape
effects. I could almost wish the glassy
meres, with their clear reflections of tree or
sky, to be permanent.

I have been looking over and making notes
of our Fir trees—we have only about a dozen
or so, I am afraid! I find that Pinus Aus-
triaca thrives better than any other here; it is
a regret to me that we did not plant numbers more of them, instead of wasting years
in trying to make Scotch Fir succeed. Spruce
never seems to do well in this part of the
country; we have two or three old Spruce
Firs which are mere poles, and some much
younger, which must be cut down to relieve
our eyes from that garden misery, a sickly
tree. Only in the "Fantaisie" are our Spruce
Firs successful, and there, from overcrowding
—for there are at least ten—they are well-

nigh spoilt. This little spot has proved good
for them, I imagine, because it was new
ground, taken in from old unbroken pasture
and well trenched. One or two others, full
and healthy, of a few years' growth, suddenly
went off last summer; it was as if a blighting
wind had scorched their branches, or lightning had seared them. I know no successful
Spruce plantations anywhere in the neigh-
bourhood. The soil is gravelly, with chalk
and flint; and sometimes trees seem to strike
their roots down into a subsoil—perhaps an
intermittent layer of greensand—and then
they go off. But this can scarcely be the only
cause that so fatally affects our Firs. About
120 miles down west, there is a group of ex-
tremely fine Spruce Firs that I have known
for the last thirty years, and when I visited
them last year I found they had all gone off
in the same way as ours here. Excelsa
Grandis flourishes equally with Pinus Aus-
triaca. One fine young plant in the " Fantaisie " was, as one says, " quite a picture "
in the summer for the perfect symmetry of
its form, and on the two topmost laterals were
just two beautifully shaped upright green

cones, crested with amber-coloured gum!
I rejoiced in this young tree during all the
season, but there is a fear since then that it
may suffer in its growth from the premature
effort. The Balm of Gilead Firs, a few of
which we put in along one side of the turf
walk, have failed entirely. I meant each to
become a little rounded beauty, like that one
planted by my father, which I remember long
years since as a wonder of aromatic greenery;
but these are grey and stunted, and they all
wear such a look of age and decay as I fear we
cannot long endure to see. The crisp leaves,
however, are as sweet when crumpled in the
hand as they ought to be. With two or three
of these piteous little trees, the branches
show, without losing stiffness, a certain tendency to droop or turn downwards at the
extremities. It is rather curious, this droop,
affected by a few individuals in a Fir
plantation! For they do not begin life with
that intention; the young tree may be just
like any other for years, when suddenly one
branch will be observed turned down, then
another and another, till finally the whole
thing is decided, and the tree becomes a

Fair Maids of February.

"weeper," as some call them. In a
large plantation in Aberdeenshire, some
years since, I knew one young Silver Fir
out of all the others that grew itself into a
drooping form, so that it seemed at last to
draw down its branches close together as
one would draw a cloak around one in the
cold. It was then ten or twelve feet high,
and now it must indeed be a remarkable
object if it has grown and drooped at the
same rate. Our Douglas Fir (Sir Bedivere)
has known this temptation to droop, but
evidently the feeling of the mass of his
branches is dead against the idea, and it will
come to nothing.

This accident or sport is common in other
trees all over the world, I suppose, and one
of the most ancient nomadic patterns of
Persian rugs depicts, on either side the Tree
of Life, the columnar Cypress and the
drooping Cypress, beside a little tomb.

In various odd nooks and corners of the
garden, I know where to find a few little
old Cephalonian Pines, all that remain out
of a number we once had. They are only
about 4 or 5 feet high, yet they were grown

from seed over a quarter of a century ago.
Like poor old useless retainers, they have
followed the fortunes of the family, and we
have become attached to one another. One
amongst the original number became a fine
specimen—and perished. The rest have
never had a chance of growing up, for every
spring their new buds are nipped, so they
remain still the same, with a sort of look of
old-young trees. I am especially interested
in the welfare of one of the Cephalonians,
who lives in an English Yew. Those
two are certainly bosom friends! The Yew
itself was only half a tree, spared, out of
charity, on what seemed a bare chance of
surviving. The Cephalonian stood near and
shivered, and lost its buds every spring,
while the Yew crept nearer and nearer, till
at last its thick dark foliage reached the little
Pine, and so grew on; and now the Yew
fairly holds it within its warm, comfortable
embrace. Some say, "What a mistake to
leave them thus!" I say, "They shall
not be parted;" so the two remain together,
and grow quite happily in each other's arms.
Oddly enough, the Pine seems to be

assimilating itself in colour, and partly in
form, with the Yew, so that it is not easy to
distinguish them. But if the Cephalonian at
last out-tops its benefactor, what will happen
then ? At times the space of ground over
which we reign seems to be very much too
small ; and I incline to envy the possession
of land, with room enough to plant; for
there can be no more engrossing interest of
its kind than to watch the growth of trees,
their manners and customs. I would plant
at once acres of Ilex Oak. What shelter
they would make ! And in a congenial soil
they would not be too slow of growth. There
should be broad bands of Beech and Oak,
and long groves of Larch, delicious in spring
for the fragrance of their green and pink-
tipped tassels. And there should be plantations of Fir—Scotch Fir, for the delight of
their healthy blue-green in youth, and for the
glory of their great red stems in age; and
Spruce Fir, with all their charm of deep
mosses underneath, and the loveliness in
spring of starry Winter-green (*Trientalis
Europæ*) and "the rathe Primrose ; " and
for the music of the winds among their

branches, and the velvet darkness of their
colour under summer skies. (*Mem.*—The
Winter-green would have to be sent us
from the North.)

Our great work of last month has been an
alteration at the east end of the garden. A
Quickset hedge, forty or fifty years old, is
moved back, so as to take in from "the
park" a bit of waste ground; the gravel path
that ran under the hedge is widened, and a
block of Laurels cut through. By this means
a turf way, leading north and south, is made
to enter the improved walk, whose chief
attraction is the border of old damask Roses.
Plum trees and Pears stand along the border
amongst the Roses, and a large perennial
yellow Lupin, in which thrushes have been
known to make their nests. In the middle
of the hedge grew a fine young Elder. I
had long promised that Elder it should never
be cut down, so when the Hawthorns were
removed the tree remained, arching across
the path to meet a Plum tree on the other
side. An Elder in full bloom is such a
beautiful thing that it is painful to feel
obliged to destroy it; but Elders have such

an unfortunate knack of appearing where they are not wanted! The birds sow Elder seeds in the clefts of trees, in chinks of walls, flower borders—all sorts of inconvenient places—now that the berries are no longer requisitioned to make Elder wine. In old-fashioned days it was worth having a cold, to enjoy a night-cap of Elder wine from the saucepan on the hob! So this one tree is preserved in honour, as compensation for those others which are no more. I am not in the least superstitious, but it *is* rather uncanny to cut down an old Elder! Eldritch legends and spells have clung to the tree in days of yore, and have even come down to our own times. I used to listen at my mother's knee, and beg again and again for the story of the fairy changeling. The interest of the story never failed, and the rhyme never tired, about the enchanted hare, who ran—

" Runie and runie the Eildon tree,
And seven times runie the Eildon tree."

According to custom, I was rather on the look-out for treasures when the old hedge was dug up, but nothing appeared excepting a huge yellow bone and a gigantic root of White Briony. The uncouth thing bore a strange resemblance to some organized being with arms and legs—something like an octopus in full swim, only twenty times as big, and yet also with a sort of human aspect! I was told it was a Mandrake (though it did not shriek on being pulled up), and so I desired it should be carefully buried, in order that the household might not be disturbed by its groans at night. In India the sounds emitted by a Mandrake in the dark night are said to be sometimes heartrending. And so the witch, in the *Masque of Queens*—

" I last night lay all alone
O' the ground to heare the mandrake grone."

I wonder if White Briony is really the true Mandrake, about which there must seriously be something mysterious. I find in the dictionary, " Mandragora (Mandrake), a powerful soporific. Mandrage, a plant said to be so called because it points out that a cave is near." I know no more, besides the wild traditions, and this vision the other day, in the twilight, of a white misshapen figure lying on the earth. There are, however, few things more exquisitely graceful than the Black and White Brionies. Black Briony is rare in our part of Buckinghamshire. In this garden three White Brionies have leave to dwell. All winter, the mystic root lies hidden, awaiting the appointed time. On a day in spring or early summer, suddenly up-springs a group of delicate pale green stalks, and they, as soon as they have seen the sun in heaven, delay not to put forth all the strength stored under the earth in the big ugly root; and before many days the green stalks have grown into a beautiful leafy plant, mantling over whatever is nearest of tree or bush, with leaves of most fanciful cut, and a thousand ringlets of circling, sensitive tendrils. By-and-by there will be a whole firmament of little star-like flowers, greenish-white in colour—all either male or female, according to the plant. In October an unhappy collapse sets in. Life ebbs fast from the flaccid stalks and tendrils, dying away, sinking down, down into the buried root, till nothing remains but a dry colourless shroud, clinging close over the supporting shrub, which scarce can breathe, till a friendly hand in due course clears the whole thing off.

I think I never saw a finer show of white Arums than we have just now. There is the grandest luxuriance of foliage, with thick tall stems, crowned by spathes in spiral lines of perfect grace. The rich texture of these flowers is marvellous; white as the drifted snow, with a lemon scent. Our success is perhaps due, not only to good management, but to what one may call imported bulbs. Four years ago they were thrown out of a garden at Cannes, as worthless rubbish, on to the road-side. I passed that way one day, while a little peasant girl was collecting some of these bulbs in her pinafore. I asked her what they were. "*Des lis!*" she said. So I immediately gathered up some for myself, and they were done up in newspapers and packed in our trunks and brought home. In grim contrast to these joyous flowers of light is the Serpent Flower, a tropical member of the Arum family. I saw it, once only, eleven years ago, in the beautiful garden of

Palazzo Orenga, at Mortola, near Ventimiglia. It grew on the edge of a ravine, under the deep shade of a low stone wall. Right up from a cluster of black-spotted leaves the centre spiral rose to about ten or twelve inches, bending over at the top into a sort of hood, like the hooded head of a cobra. The creature—flower I cannot say—took the attitude exactly of a snake preparing to spring, the body marked and spotted the same as a snake, with the hood greyish-brown. The whole thing seemed something more than a good imitation only of the reptile whose name it bears. The first glance gave a sort of shock, as if on a sudden one had become aware of the actual presence at one's feet of a deadly serpent; and yet the terrifying object is, I believe, used by the Indians as an antidote to snake-bite.

All over the Olive grounds of the same country where the Serpent Arum is acclimatized, about this time or early in March, appear the little brown " Sporacci "—tiny hooded Arums of quaint form, little odd monks with yellow tongues hanging out (Arum Arisarum). My window is full of Paper

Narcissus—Narcissus is Remembrance; and for the sake of past days, I love it—they succeed a set of blue Roman Hyacinths, dear also from association, and beautiful in their full tones of blue and green. The perfume of both flowers brings back vividly the sweet South, where I knew them wild. I must end with a little bit out of a letter sent me from that southern land which has the power to create lovers of Nature:—

"I am longing for sunshine, to bring to life all the flowers I am watching for near the torrent beds. My ignorance of flowers has this advantage, that each leaf is a mystery to me, and I know not what flower it frames, so each will be a surprise as it appears."

MARCH.

"Out of the Snow, the Snowdrop—
Out of Death comes Life." . . .

DAVID GRAY.

VI.

MARCH.

March 9.—We are rejoicing in the fulfilment of a long-felt wish, and at last we possess a rookery! There are the nests, seven of them, in the Elms, in full view of our east windows. The grand old trees have always seemed to us a most tempting position for the rooks, who themselves have half thought so too. But it has taken them long to come to a decision. On many a spring morning for these eleven years past have we observed them settling upon the trees in hundreds. But after a short interval

of noise and clamour, they would rise and
depart. They were only coquetting a
little with us, or bent on kindling delusive
hopes. "Ill blows the wind that profits
nobody," however; so the storm of April 29
last year, which uprooted some of our best
trees, laid low also part of a neighbouring
rookery. The shock seems to have decided
the rooks, and to have won their confidence
in our noble 300-year-old Elms. The seven
nests were begun and nearly built in about
as many days. How busy the old rooks are!
And how, with no hands and only one beak,
they can make up those neat bundles of moss
and dry grass, just like potatoes, that we
see them carrying to line the nests with, is
difficult to understand. During the rough
snowy weather no work was done; but a
rook or two sat all day just above the nests
on the very topmost twigs, swaying in the
wind, as if to watch and test their security.
One evening at dusk, after the rooks had gone
off for the night, an inquisitive starling came
peeping about. He flew up from his own
lower range, visiting every nest; made a
minute inspection inside and out, and then

decamped in a great hurry, afraid of being
found out.

Near the great Elms, but far below the
new black colony, is the dovecote. Beautiful
white fantail pigeons, varied by two or three
purple-necked greys, here live joyous lives.
On the steep, heather-thatched roof they
preen, and coo, and make love together, or
rise with sudden dash into the air, and
wheel in circling flight over the lawns and
flower-beds. On sunny days, when they
pass and repass the house, swift gleams flash
along the rooms within; brown oak panel-
lings reflecting back the sunshine from their
silver plumes. Often, through long summer
afternoons, will these bright shadows come
and go upon the walls, like visions of happy
ghosts upon the wing. It is not all poetry,
however, with our fantails, I am afraid ; for
the handsomest of them all choked himself
with too greedily swallowing a slug one day,
and was found stretched dead upon the lawn.
Sometimes a poor tailless fugitive, escaped
from the nearest public-house shooting-
match, will take refuge with our pigeons
and feed shyly with them for a day or

so; but only one ever remained, and she went to live with the bantam cock, whose pert little wife had deserted him.

The day has been cold, with scattered flakes of snow falling; and now, in the grey still evening, the air is suffused with a certain splendid sobriety of colouring, if it may be so described. The turf has lost that living green it showed a month ago, for since then bitter winds have swept the garden; the Yews look dark and sombre, dark pyramids and lines; the older Yews, of large and natural growth, are powdered over with dim gold-dust. Such profuse bloom on the Yews seems to soften their blackness. Beyond the Yew hedges' dusky outline glows a richer green of Laurel, Cedar, and Firs, with the russet sheen of Beech, half seen between the budding fulness of Thorn and Laburnum. Beyond all stand the Elms; they form a background of infinite delicacy, purpling under that nameless change, more felt than seen, which the turn of the year has brought. Nearer home, in this pale evening light, the hoary old garden walls, with here and there a ruddier tint of redder brick, or faintest

blush upon them of Pyrus Japonica, join their
mellow tones to the intense but quiet colour
of the hour. A mass of common sweet-
scented white Clematis, whose summer
glory has long since melted into a softly
shaded cloud of thin withered stalks, hides
one pillar of the central iron gate, and half
enwreathes a sculptured vase above; sere
leaves of grassy wild things break the
straight line of mossy, lichened coping.
Timid thrushes with spotted breast, and
little hedge-sparrows in sober brown, appear
upon the lawn, since labour for the day is
done and the garden is deserted. A tomtit,
quaintly liveried, has made the square-
topped Yewen hedge his hunting-ground.
(Yewen was the pretty old word in Spen-
ser's time: may we not revive it?) But
now a bold gay blackbird leaps up upon the
stone ball that surmounts the ivied corner of
the wall. His jet-black plumage and "the
golden dagger of his bill" give just that
touch of strength wanted to complete the
consonance of lovely colour. By-and-by he
will be down again upon the grass to flirt his
tail and flout the thrushes till he remains

alone, master of the field. This is a dull
time for the cock birds all over the place.
Awhile ago they had such games of an evening on the lawn! chasing each other in and
out between the Yews and Box tree, and
every blackbird had two hens to play hide
and seek with. But now the lawful wives
are sitting, and there's an end of the fun.

The garden has been cold and joyless ever
since March 4. It is true that morning after
morning, about sunrise, a treat for the eye
has been prepared by the Crocus beds with a
succession of white frosts, but it is one could
well be spared. Meanwhile, it certainly is
the prettiest sight imaginable, these Crocuses
thrown lightly, as it were, upon the frosted
turf in garlands of amethyst and amber.
The rime, covering up all varied greens and
browns of earth and grass with a veil of
pearly grey, gives a most pure and charming
result. If you look quite near—at the
purple wreath especially—the flowers seem
all dipped in pounded sugar, crystallized for
a fairy's feast. Except this pretty morning
show, there is as yet but little joy. Fewer
flowers than in January even, and such as

are willing to bloom cast down on the
ground. Primroses and the earliest Daffodils
are thus laid low, conquered by overmaster-
ing cold. Violets, too, which before the frost
began were almost more perfumed and of
finer bloom than ever I remember, are
pinched and shrunken. Snowdrops also
failed, before the severe frost, destroyed
untimely by excessive rain. The Snowflake
(*Leucojum vernum*) appeared earlier than
usual, and I look forward to the summer
Snowflake later on. These lovely flowers
came from an eyot on the Thames, where
they grow wild. A fine double Snowdrop
played an amusing little freak. The southern
face of a Yew hedge under which it grew
had, I suppose, gradually overgrown the
plant, so its stalks had to preternaturally
lengthen themselves, growing up within the
hedge till forth peeped the flowers from
various little interspaces, as if the Yew
itself were breaking out into Snowdrops!
One of these long stems measured sixteen
inches, and the blossoms, larger than common, looked as if they enjoyed the joke.

Few indeed are the flowers to be recorded

in bloom. There is a pink tuft or two of Dog's-tooth Violet (long lines of these, if there were space sufficient, would make great show). Grape Hyacinths (looking very unripe) are an inch or so above-ground. The sweet little dwarf Daffodil, with bent head, smiles to itself in the accustomed place. A few Polyanthuses, small blue Periwinkles, mixed with yellow Primroses; Pulmonaria, seared and pinched; blue Scilla, in niggard clumps, quite unlike its usual bounteous, radiant beauty. These, with bushes of rosy Ribes, checked but ready to break into bloom, are about all we can boast. There are, indeed, the Crocuses, whose best days, however, will soon be ended. The mixed border of these, in three colours—yellow, white, and lilac—would have been perfect had our friends the field-mice, instead of choosing the lilac alone for their own private consumption, shown more impartiality. Their taste is certainly remarkable, for the yellow were the fattest bulbs.

Mar. 19.—After a day of rain it is wonderful how quickly Daffodils and Primroses have picked themselves up. The Grape Hyacinths have grown two inches since morning, and begun to colour in proportion, or so at least it seems; and tiny golden buds, unperceived before, burgeon all over the Kerria. Although Daffodils as yet are few, there is already a Polyanthus Narcissus unfolded, and a few Narcissus of deep orange-yellow have arisen behind the lilac winter Irises. The Apricot bloom is chiefly brown, but all will not be lost. On the Peach trees there are buds, and some expanded blooms of heavenly pink. I find a curious small deception has been practised upon me by a plant in the east border. I had often observed two patches of greenish worn-out-looking moss there, and at last inquired of the Gardener the reason of their being permitted. He pointed out that it was not moss, but the green bare roots of a Violet, which I am well acquainted with when its disguise is thrown off. It is a pied Dog Violet, from Villa Clara, Baveno. We have had it now for some years. The flower is scentless, striped white and purple, of large size, on a long stalk. But flower and leaf are yet a long way off.

7

The pruning and trimming of all the Ivy walls and festoons have been done. The result for the time is as ugly as it is desirable. Ivy grows so lavishly here that it has to be kept well in hand, and many whom it favours less have said they envied us our Ivy. More than once we have had to choose between some tree or a canopy of Ivy. It is like a beautiful carpet underneath a long row of Elms, where nothing else would grow; indeed, wherever there happen to be bits too overshadowed for grass or otherwise unsatisfactory, we put in Ivy; it is sure to understand, and to do what is required. My favourite sort is the wild English Ivy, and no other has a right to grow on the house. Its growth is slow and sure; it always grows to beauty, and never to over-richness. The loveliness of its younger shoots and of the deeply cut leaves might inspire either poet or painter! To either I would say, Wherever on your tree, or fence, or house-wall you find it beginning to spring, cherish it; for years it will do no harm, and if you are true to your art, and therefore know that small things are

not too small for you, it will repay your love
a hundredfold. Wild Ivy is best where it
comes up of itself; it clings then so close and
flat. A thrush sat on her nest, built on quite
the outside of a Holly, two feet from the
ground, while the men were at work pruning an Ivy wall—large swathes of Ivy falling
close to her. She had faith in us, and never
feared.

Our grove of white Arums in the greenhouse is still a fine sight—plants from four
to five feet high, with enormous leaves.
The spathes, however, though fine, are less
so than at first, when many of them measured
over eight inches across. The Maréchal
Niel Rose will not give us this season
anything like the six hundred great yellow
roses we have had from him these last
three years. He seems to be failing a little,
somehow. But every morning I have a
foretaste of summer in the glowing heap
of beautiful roses of several kinds, brought
in to me before breakfast. And with them
there are Gloxinias, marvellous in their
size and splendour of deep colouring.
They are succeeding a lot of most curious-

looking Tydæas—orange and dusky pink, profusely spotted. Both these flowers surprise one by the length of time they remain fresh when cut.

APRIL.

"To the Wise a Fact is True Poetry, and the most Beautiful of Fables."—EMERSON.

VII.

APRIL.

Of Daffodils—Coltsfoot—An Archangel—Gold Wrens
and the little Vedova.

April 9.—The garden is full of Daffodils.
Yellow flowers and green leaves form a
most beautiful combination of colours when
laid on by Nature's hand. Every part of
the garden now has its show of single or
double Daffodils, and yet there is not one
too many. Lovely always, they are loveliest,
perhaps, when growing in the grass. There,
"the green world they live in" shows them
off better than when surrounded by garden
mould. Excepting one large single flowering plant under the east wall, our finest
Daffodils grow in the cool north border.

One thinks of "Enid" in her faded silk,
like a blossom "that lightly breaks a faded
flower-sheath" when the Daffodils appear.
Indeed, one can scarcely look on them, in
their beauty, without recalling the lines of
some familiar quotation; mine shall only be
from the children's nursery song-book—

> "Daffy-down-dilly has come up to town
> In a yellow petticoat and a green gown."

(Poor Daffodilla! for yellow is jealousy, and
green is forsaken.) The old jingle paints
well enough the Daffodil's outside. Whatever else may lie within the golden depth of
her cup and about her silken petals, all the
poetry of the Daffodil has been said and sung
from old, old days, up to our own time, by
those happy few whose thoughts shape themselves in verse. Soon there will be a blooming of many varieties in the garden, but at
this moment only three abound, and of these
I hardly know which most to praise. There
is the single variety, with rather narrow,
almost pointed petals, and trumpet tube of a
deeper shade of yellow; I cannot distinguish
this one from Narcissus Incomparabilis of

the Riviera. Then there is the semi-double
(old Parkinson's Narcissus Major, "confined
to the gardens of the curious"), which I
sometimes think a still more handsome
flower, from its rich folded depths of colour.
Its prime, however, lasts but a few days;
the full tube seems then to overspread
and split, and a confusion of doubleness
ensues which mars its perfect form. Then
there is the old real Daffodil—quite apart
from the so-called Lent Lily—with very
pale, broad-leaved corolla, and true Narcis-
sus-shaped cup. When this doubles itself
there is again a loss of grace. I call it the
real Daffodil, because years ago, when that
was a flower not thought so much of, this,
as I remember, was the usual kind seen in
gardens. I believe in those days the Daffodil
—whose very name is music in our ears
—was considered almost a vulgar (!) flower;
"it was so very common." Now it is so
common in another way, one could half
wish that it—with the Sunflower—had remained undiscovered, or only bloomed to
grace old cottage garden plots, or as the
Lent Lily, in wild woodland ways, for the

delight of simple village children. Is it
fault or failing in human nature that inclines
us to turn from things that all the world
admires? I only know that, somehow, one
loves one's own love to be for one's self
alone! and I do not care to see cartfuls of
Daffodils sent up to London. . . . There is a
part of the garden on the north side which
just now gives me strange pleasure. There
we leave the borders to grow pretty much
how they will. In summer on one side
there is a green forest of Male-Fern, Bramble,
wild Ivy, and low-grown Berberis; but at
this time the scene is different. Great double
Daffodils rest their golden heads upon inter-
lacing red-brown Fern and branching glossy
Berberis. A few shafts of narrow blue-
green leaves pierce through and amongst
the brown and burnt-sienna colour; Pulmonaria—taking heart after all the withering
frosts—breaks into clouds of flower, all blue
and pink, with dusks of mottled leaf between.
And among the Pulmonaria crops up by
chance, in the humblest way, a healthy
beautiful Archangel, or Dead Nettle, set
with blossoms downy white.

"More springs in the garden than the gardener ever sowed," is an old saying. Just the other side the walk there chances—who knows how?—a charming little plant which curiously attracts me. Unlike "the small Celandine," it never had a poet, so far as I know, to sing its praise, although the Painter-poet of England—William Blake—disdained not to immortalize it. In his illustrations to the Book of Job it occurs, the character of the flowers unmistakably given by a few master-touches. Yet this little Coltsfoot is full of interest, and the little satiny sun-flower that crowns each pinkish fleshy flower-stalk is, in its way, quaintly unique. The *specimen* (*vide* Dryasdust) in our north border has rooted partly under and amongst the lowest leaves of an Aucuba, partly in the Box edging. I think it has been in a vague way not unknown to me for many past seasons, but I have passed it unob-servantly, only perhaps remarking to myself, "Ah, there you are again!" One day, how-ever, it drew down my attention to look more closely, and since, it has had sometimes half-a-dozen visits in the day. I wished to

see if there were any set hours for its unfolding and closing; it seemed so odd to
find the little flowers fast shut at near 8 a.m.,
with the sunshine bright upon them. Then
I found they did not open till between 11
and 12 mid-day. One placed in water, at
a south window, opened itself wide before
nine in the morning, and at noon the small
yellow disc was spread so broad that its
rays turned over the other way at the edges.
You could scarcely find on any flower's face
an expression of more serene content. Then
both the growing flowers and the one in the
window began to close at precisely the same
time—about ten minutes to 4 p.m.; and the
closing process with both only came to an end
at near 6. This slowness may have been,
perhaps, because the flowers were then all
rather past their first youth. In grey cloudy
weather they hardly unclosed at all. The
spot where this Coltsfoot has chosen to grow
must be unsympathetic, for after the early
morning a light chequered shade of Holly,
from over the way, veils in some degree its
coveted sun supply. When its time comes
the little flower dies very prettily; it only

changes to a dull saffron hue, and then shuts up for ever.

The all too brief delight of hearing the birds sing in the evening is not at its best; about seven they begin. The other day, at 6.30, scarce a note was heard through all the garden. The rooks were cawing in a whisper their hoarse good-nights; two wood-pigeons answered each other from trees far apart in the fields, with an interrupted chant—"slow to begin and never ending." Suddenly, a little before seven—about three minutes before—one after another the thrushes awoke into song. The whole air echoed and resounded with their music. It was the same time, precisely, as on the day before. How do they tell the hour thus to a minute? Not certainly by the clock; for seven struck from the village church tower just three minutes after the concert began. Can it be the first star appearing that sets for them the moment to begin? Looking up, the pole star shone from heaven right overhead. Does some "wise thrush," sitting on a topmost branch, with full bright orbs turned heavenwards, mark this sudden diamond in the sky,

and then at once pour forth his flood of liquid melody, the signal for his fellows waiting round to take up the song? We watched near the Douglas Fir, I and the satin-coated colley dog; he listened too, lying on the grass, rather bored but patient, with ears alert; and twilight deepened, and star after star stole out upon the dusk, while the orange west grew dim and changed, and louder still re-echoed the ecstatic numbers from every bush and tree, and from many a hedgerow in the fields beyond. In all this multitude of bird voices not a discord intervenes; it is an orchestra turned to one key, and the fuller the tones of the unnumbered instruments, the deeper and more entire is the concord. How is it done? There is no conductor with his baton! . . . But the dinner-bell rings, and we must leave the concert and all its sweet-throated minstrels in full song, and the garden, with its refined and lovely influences of perfect harmony, its budding trees and tuneful thickets of Fir and Laurel, to the Daffodils and the stars. The contrast is somewhat gross, of roast mutton and lighted lamps! . . . But to those

who prefer their Currant bushes to the songs
of "God's poet hid in foliage green," what
can be said? I do not believe such persons
exist.

The Sweet Briar hedge along the walk
leading to the wicket-gate in the entrance-
drive begins to scent the air. We do not
make enough of such a treasure as Sweet
Briar is. Some day we must plant some
near the windows, for pleasant perfume after
rain. It is a favourite idea, too obscure to
be a doctrine or even a theory, that the
sweet smells of flowers, and aromatic leaves,
and all kinds of green things have a certain
virtue for different conditions of health.
Here are a few examples, and I am afraid
I do not know many more: To smell wild
Thyme will renew the spirits and vital
energy in long walks under an August sun.
The pure, almost pungent scent of Tea Rose
Maréchal Niel is sometimes invigorating in
any lowness of mind or body. Sweet Briar
promotes cheerfulness. Yellow Bedstraw
(*Galium verum*), Cowslip, Wallflower, Damask and pink China Roses, Plum blossom, and notably Sweet Gale or Bog Myrtle,

and wild white Honeysuckle refresh the
spirits; while the smell of ground Ivy, Char-
lock, Woodruff, Rosemary, and fresh-cut grass
seems to be a refreshment to the body.
Hawthorn is very doubtful, and Lime blossom is dreamy. These scents are "transparent," and are also, except the two first,
more or less uncertain, to be caught on
the wing, as it were. The more positive
and "opaque" scents, such as those of the
Gardenia, Lilies, Narcissus, Jonquil, etc.,
seem less potent for the spirits than for the
body. The subject is full of indistinctness,
since that which is life to one may be death
to many. I have known an instance of even
white Sweet Peas and white Pink being
unendurable, and yet both are what I call
"transparent." There may also be a system
of mixed flowers. Small scarlet Nasturtium
and lemon-scented Pelargonium are good
together, and seem to have a pleasant effect
on the mind, and as the venerable Parkinson says, they "make a delicate Tussimussie,
or Nosegay, both for sight and scent." The
large Italian white Jasmine, mixed with
Marie Louise Violets, is comforting. Alto-

gether I think the idea may be something more than a mere fantastic whim.*

April 17.—This morning, before 8 o'clock, the whole garden felt like spring. The turf was brightly green and shining with dew, and birds, and grass, and flowers were unconsciously at ease and happy for the moment under the warm sunlight. The unwonted warmth made a robin so bold and confident, that he flew up against me in the most playful way, and then perched on a young Beech, flapping his little wings with a merry twinkle in his eye. All about and in and out the Stone Pine, to them one huge world of insect life, flitted a pair of golden crested wrens, as busy as possible,

---

* Nearly twelve months after writing thus about healthful Flower-scents, I found in Austen's "Treatise of Fruit-trees," 1657, a curious confirmation of my idea, which appears, indeed, to be an old one. He writes, "Health is preserved by pleasant and wholesome Odors, and perfumes found in the garden of Fruit-trees, . . . from the blossomes of *all the Fruit-trees*, . . . which are not simply Healthfull, but are accompted cordiall ; chearing and refreshing the heart and vitall spirits."—*Note, April,* 1884.

8

the flutter of their tiny wings making just as much sound as might two butterflies. The sun glanced now and then, for a moment, on the cock-bird's golden streak, the hen held a filmy white insect of some kind in her bill, and would on no account show the way to her nest, so long as she was watched. It was unkind, I fear, to tease so minute a creature, and I soon went another way; and then both wrens made a little rush into the brambly ivy-smothered trunk of the tree. We refrain from too curiously searching for the nest, though I think the young family would be worth seeing! In the morning light a host of single Daffodils shone like pale gold; double white Wind-flowers have begun to bloom (there grows a yellow wild one * not far from us, but I have only seen it after it had been transplanted into a garden), and many kinds of Narcissus. The Pasque-flower has been put out of its reckoning by the unusually early Easter; it is only just

---

* Anemone Ranunculoides is alluded to. The gardener of the garden where I saw it assured me it grew wild in a little wood close by, but I did not myself see it wild.

in bud. The grass walk in the Fantaisie
was too heavy with dew to be pleasant, so
I only looked across the gate at the Narcissus
and flaming star Anemones. In the clear
sunlight, lilac patches of Aubrietia, side by
side with clean white Arabis, seem doubly
charming.

How eagerly one seizes all possible points
of beauty in such a severe trying season ! I
never before remember our having to water
the garden in April ; it has been, however,
quite necessary, for as yet only two slight
April showers have fallen, and the clumps of
Narcissus Poeticus were failing. Tulips are
flowering with stalks barely one inch long,
and Crown Imperials half miss their usual
" stately beautifulness." One day of soft
warm rain would set all right, and give us
an almost Roman spring, so suddenly would
the garden become clothed in bloom, and the
leaves burst out upon the trees. King-cups
begin to glass themselves in our narrow
watercourse, and reeds to thicken greenly
along the brink. The long line of Primroses
along the *Allée Verte* is a sad failure. As soon
as the flowers open they are beheaded by

those cruel chaffinches. This is how the
little painted traitors behave all the while
they are supposed to be gaily building their
dainty nests! Such wholesale execution is,
I believe, the result of this very dry weather.
They cut off the flowers to get at the small
drop of moisture or honey in the calyx. I
forgive the chaffinches without any difficulty,
only wishing that other people could be as
easily pardoned; but when the rooks are
poisoned and our new hopes of a rookery
nearly frustrated, it is hard to be very for-
giving! Some short-sighted farmer has
done this cruel deed. The poor rooks
dropped on our own land on the grass under
their nests. Several of their young must
have perished miserably, and the deserted
nests look very sad. Still we think enough
young remain to save the rookery. The
Florentine yellow Tulips are in bloom. How
far more lovely to the unhorticultural eye
are these wild kinds, with their graceful
bending stalks, than those the Tulip's cultiva-
tion has so well succeeded in stiffening—
with all their grand colour! On the 7th
appeared, as I knew she would sooner or

. later, the little "Vedova" Iris of Florence.
Under the south wall, where we did not
think to seek, there she was, for the first
time after these eight years' seclusion. And
still she wears her weeds of green and black.
The roots have increased and thrown up
quantities of leaves. These leaves are not
rounded like those of the Spanish Iris and
other long narrow kinds ; they are four-sided,
with sharp angles, very strong, and have a
sharp point at the end.

MAY.

"Pale crocuses have come before her;
  Wild birds her welcome sing;
Ten thousand loving hearts adore her,
  The grey world's darling, Spring."

W. M. ELTON.

VIII.

MAY.

Of Cherry Blossoms—the Nightingale's " Melodious Noise "—Of Broken Stones, etc., etc., etc.

May 6.—The month of May would be Heaven upon earth if only it came in August or September, when summer mostly begins ! but such cold, hard weather as we have had spoils sadly our enjoyment of the blossom trees and all the pleasures of spring. There have been just one or two sweet days, when the white Cherry orchards shone softly against a sky of serenest blue; days when we did but revel in the joyous present, forgetting quite that ever it could be that " rough winds do shake the darling buds of May." Alas ! all too soon our dream is

dispelled ; dark clouds arise, and we see
" Heaven's gold complexion dimmed," and
the orchard grass strewn with pearly wreck.
The Cherry tree's magic season is at an end ;
it seemed to last scarcely longer than a day.
With the first hot shafts of April's sun it
startles into bloom, shaken out in snow-
wreaths all over the tree, a waste of most
lavish loveliness. It is something gained,
once in the twelvemonth's round of common-
place, if only for a moment to stand beside
a Cherry tree in blossom. The blue sky
looks infinitely far off, seen through such a
maze of flowery myriads. And now Apple
blossoms are coming on in rosy swift succession. How beautiful they are ! and is it not
time that water-colour artists should cease to
weary, by attempting so vainly to pourtray
them ? (This only by the way.) They have
the merit of lasting just long enough for us to
enjoy them well ; yet beautiful as they are,
I do not know if they can ever quite compare
with the frail short-lived cherry. If the
Espaliers in the kitchen garden alongside the
middle walk would but flower together all at
once, that walk in May would be better than

any picture-gallery. But our gallery walls
perversely decorate themselves only a little
bit at a time. One bit, at a corner of the
cross-walks, is now in full perfection. A
faint delicious perfume steals out through
the iron gate to the flower-garden, inviting
as one passes by, to turn and peep within.
There are the trained leafless branches
covered thick with knots of flower. They
open very deliberately, and there abide for a
little happy while, self-conscious, round, and
pink, and firm ; then there comes a setting of
delicate green around the flowers ; and then
the Apple tree in bloom is one of earth's
loveliest sights. Apple blossom must be
added to my pharmacopœia of sweet smells.
To inhale a cluster of Blenheim Orange gives
back youth for just half a minute after. It is
not merely that with the perfume the heart
goes back to remembered times—it is a real,
absolute elixir! Our young Siberian Crab
trees are like great white bouquets; and
behind the pigeon-house there is a wonder
of Japanese Apple (*Pyrus malus floribunda*).
It is like a fountain of flowers, tossing its
pink flower-laden branches in every direc-

tion. Blue Periwinkles creep over the
ground underneath it. In the autumn I shall
hope to plant several more of these lovely
trees somewhere on the lawn, where we may
see and enjoy them from the windows. And
now the Primrose—

> " Lady of the springe,
> The lovely flower that first doth show her face ;
>   Whose worthy prayse the pretty byrds do syng,
> Whose presence sweet the wynter's colde doth chase,"

has ceased to glad us " with worldes of new
delightes." She is on the wane, " with her
bells dim "—as old Ben Jonson said ; but I
should not call them bells. She dies upon
a bed of vivid green amidst tall grasses and
her own thick-coming leaves, as stars grow
pale before the dawn. And we are faithless
to her beauty in the presence of other, fresher
loveliness ; and we care not though the
Primrose is dead.

The Tulips in the parterr—it is the older
and prettier way to spell it without an "e"
at the end—are now the chief ornament of
the garden and the delight of my eyes.
Timely rains strengthened the stalks to

rise to their full height, and there are the beds
now, a blaze of scarlet and yellow splendour.
There are tall Tulips and short Tulips, rose
and crimson, scarlet and orange Tulips,
striped and dashed, and brown and white,
and every shade of Tulip colour. A few grow
between little box and golden Arbor Vitæ
bushes, and all the beds are deeply fringed
with Crocus leaves. I am aware that as a
matter of the highest principle, Tulips are
seldom mixed; the colours are usually
arranged separately. Long experience has
taught me, however, to have nothing to do
with principles—in the garden. Little else
than a feeling of entire sympathy with the
diverse characters of your plants and flowers
is needed for "art in the garden." If sympathy be there, all the rest comes naturally
enough. No brighter, gayer garden scene
can be imagined than on a sunny morning,
turning the corner of a clipped Yew—
buttressed out from the house—to come upon
the parterr, decked in all its gay brilliancy of
Tulips. The sculptured stone pillar rises
from a little mound of Stonecrop in the
centre, often with a pigeon or a thrush

pluming itself on the top. Suddenly the little
flock of fantail pigeons with whistling wings
descend among the many-coloured brilliants,
and there, in the emerald, dewy interspaces,
they strut and play in their pride and purity
of whiteness. My favourite Parrot Tulips do
not as yet make much way; the lack of sunshine keeps their buds green. It was in
Venice, years ago, that first I fell in love
with Tulips such as these. On the marble
altars of one of the great Jesuit churches
were vases filled with Parrot Tulips, all cut-
edged and gold and scarlet-splashed. The
cloister garden behind the church was full
of them. It is a strange disorderly beauty,
and sometimes draggles and hangs its untidy head like a Bell-flower, and sometimes
flaunts it up full in the sun's face. There
are Forget-me-nots in many parts of the
garden; their long smoke-like lines of
turquoise are specially pleasing. Two
square beds in the entrance court, set
between the black Yews, are also a success—
Forget-me-not, flecked with pink Saponaria
—they give the idea of blue mist touched
by the sunset. In the Fantaisie, bushes of

orange-coloured Berberis Darwinii are in
great perfection of bloom. There is something peculiarly delightful in the way they
have of spreading the earth with orange,
while yet the laden boughs above own no
apparent loss. The orange colour contrasts
well also with a chance lot of purple Honesty,
which has grouped itself round a smooth-
stemmed young Mulberry at the end of the
turf walk. The walk itself is very bright,
with an irregular bordering of white and
pink Phlox Nelsoni—a Cheiranthus, or
a deep blue Gentian, here and there. The
little low-growing Phlox comes in exquisite
patches of colour all over the garden. When
in flower, the plant itself—which is strag-
gling and rather ugly—is completely hid by
a flat mass of close-set bloom. In these
" gardens on a level " I am always wishing
for rockeries and little low terraces, which
should be all draped with Convolvulus
Mauristiana, Phlox Nelsoni, Aubretia, and
wild Ivy and Alyssum, or something yellow.
I should not much care for many rare Alpine plants, I think; though a surprise of
the kind here and there would be charm-

ing. Colour I must have, and plenty of
it, to rejoice the eye and make glad the
heart.

A tract of wild, savage scenery, six square
yards in extent, is in contemplation at the
afforested end of the Fantaisie. Already
one or two large pieces of a sort of con-
glomerate have been conveyed here, and are
frowning in an open space amongst the wild
Bluebells. There is a background of dark
Arbor Vitæ, and beyond, the pleasant fields
are seen, with the cows and Elms and an
Oak tree. There exists a certain necessity
for feature in this flattest of all places! The
Yew hedges and pyramids have done much
to give character to the flower garden, and
now there must be rocks for variety.

A heap of fragments of an old headless
statue lies near the rocky waste; part of a
sitting figure—a hand and a foot—and lumps
of heavy drapery, overlaid in beautiful green
velvet of moss. Very forlorn the broken
stones look, and I cannot decide to make
them into rockwork. None now know whom
the statue in its day was meant to represent
—probably a garden goddess, Flora or Po-

mona—but its history is rather quaint, if not touching. It was beloved by a lady who lived here once, and hated by her sister, and according as each for the time reigned in the other's absence, it was set up in a niche of the garden wall, or cast down with ignominy. At last the sister who loved the statue died, and then it was broken to pieces, and flung down a well. It was fished up again long after, before our time. Tradition tells of another statue, an image of Old Time, that stood or sat at one end of the pond in " the park," but of this there remains no trace.

I am happy in the possession of two long-desired flowers, which seem now to be settling down in their new abode. One is the pale-blue Star Anemone Apennina, common in the Ilex woods of Frascati ; the other, the lovely purplish-brown Fritillary (*Meleagris*), found wild in river meadows near us. Fritillary is no easy word for poetry, yet it is named by at least one poet. Matthew Arnold, in his " Thyrsis," says—

" I know what white, what purple fritillaries

9

> The grassy harvest of the river-fields,
> Above by Ensham, down by Sandford, yields."

I think no other flower of any kind can compare with it in finish and exquisite grace of form. The purplish, dove-like colour I believe to be the same described in old French as " colombette."

May 15.—To-day, amid the brilliant green of new leaves and the singing and twittering of a thousand birds in the sun's warm glow, one keeps saying to oneself—

" Spring, the sweet spring, is the year's pleasant king,"

or some such old snatch of songs that seem to wander upon the soft sweet air. Ah, yes, "the year's pleasant king"! and yet our spring is a beautiful spirit, and she has been hovering about us ; but now, to-day, she has set her feet upon the earth, and there is a great triumph of verdure on the trees and on the grass ; and Apple trees meet her in fulness of bloom, and May-buds are swelling on the Thorns to make up for lost time ; and all the edges of meadow-grass are jewelled with little gems of purple, and blue, and red, and the broad fields shine in silver and gold.

The short reign of Narcissus Poeticus has
begun; our large old clumps down one side
of the Broad Walk are not so fine as usual;
frosts and cold heavy rains laid the leaves of
some of them, and sometimes turned them
yellow; but within the walled garden the
clumps are as beautiful as ever—throngs of
long-stalked silvery flowers, stiff and firm,
with the stiffness and strength of perfect
health. Narcissus Poeticus is lovely; and
we need not trouble to know if it be the
very flower named by Theocritus, Virgil, and
Ovid. The east border, though not much
varied as yet, is gay and full of promise.
There are double pale yellow Ranunculus
(the Swiss meadow kind), and bunches of
Heartsease, violet and brown Auriculas, sheets
of double white Anemones, and the Riviera
double scarlet—which, however, never with
us comes scarlet, but only dull red; Tulips,
Stonecrops, Kingspear, Phlox Nelsoni, double
King's-cups, and Bachelors' Buttons, a patch
of Gentians at the south angle of the wall,
with yellow Corydalis Lutea peering out of
chinks in the old bricks above. Crowds of
Lilies are springing up in the background, with

purple Iris and Pæonies in bud. Solomon's
Seal (Lady's Signet) in many nooks and
corners unfolds its curious club-shaped leaf-
buds, and all its bells will soon be hung.
Pansies, under the south wall, make a bright
display; there are three large oblong beds—
lilac, yellow, and deep royal purple; also a
round bed of semi-double Anemones, whose
scarlet colour, about mid-day, is actually
dazzling; and one of Ranunculus not yet
opened. Behind these beds, against the wall,
are white Irises, almost ready to bloom, and
several clusters of the garden Star of Beth-
lehem—valuable in its way, but not nearly
so pretty as the wild sort, and most precise
in its daily system of early closing and late
opening.

Between the tennis-court and the little
lawn belonging to the Firs and Cedar, the
walk winds along beside a close of chosen
trees—Plane, Silver Birch, pink Thorns,
variegated Maple, etc., all in their pleasant
time of youth, having been planted only a
little over eleven years. Portugal Laurel
and Box mingle with them in deeper shades.
Next the walk are Sweet Briar and well-

berried Aucubas; one Aucuba is still covered
with scarlet fruit and golden leaves. There
is yellow Spanish Broom, and tall trees of
white Broom wave long white plumes, leaning over the path. White Broom, they say,
is "the Juniper tree" that Elijah sat down
under. If so, the shade must have been but
scanty! Soon the path turns past a Yew-
tree, and becomes the Primrose Walk, along
under the line of Elms.

On the left are the *Allée Verte*, and the
dovecote, and small orchard, bounded by
Beech and Yew, and crossed by flower-
bordered smooth-shaven grassy ways, all
leading to the Broad Walk; on the right a
little hidden path passes on to the oft-named
Fantaisie. Just before coming to the Yew
tree, on warm days ever since the beginning
of the month, one is met and surrounded by
a wonderful cloud of fragrance! One looks
round in vain for some bed of flowers whence
should proceed so powerful a scent. It is
like the finest Jasmine and Citron, and I
know not what of sweetest unknown incense.
It is the greeting sent out from a dense mass
of Spurge Laurel (*Daphne pontifia*), with un-

obtrusive green flowers in full bloom. It grows over a bit of the Iris bank, and its great luxuriance proves how it loves a southern aspect.

In our garden the birds have divided the kingdom amongst them, and in this half is the portion that fell to the reed sparrow. He keeps the Silver Birch alive with his busy note. Landmarks, known only to themselves, divide the territory of the reed sparrow from the realm of the nightingale. The fiery-hearted nightingale! He sings all day, and his song makes the night glorious. The north-east region of the garden he keeps for himself alone. There, on still evenings, long after sunset, is heard the faint barking of distant watch-dogs, or the sound of horses' hoofs on the road. There is his favourite tree—the grand old Thorn—where, as he sings, he may press a thousand thorns into his breast! There, across the hedge, he sees the meadow with a shimmering yellow of Cowslips all over it—if Cowslips be his desire, as is said. There, not too far off, is the straight long railroad—and he loves the thunder of the train, and the red, fire-spitting

engine; but late in the night, when there
is dark and death-like silence among the
trees, then the nightingale claims possession of the whole, and all the garden is
his own. I know not if the nightingale's
song be melancholy or joyous. His voice
has all the pathos of the finest things, and
in the broken notes we feel that not all
nor half his soul is uttered, and in each
splendid fragment there is the sense of
endless possibilities; this, I think, is the
secret of the nightingale's incomparable
charm.

I have omitted to mention amongst our
Pansies, a very choice kind. It is a curious
burnt-brown colour, like the once fashionable
"Paris brûlé." We name it Highcliff, after
the place from whence we had it first. Two
large pink Oleanders in the greenhouse will
soon be blossoming all over. We tried them
last year in the open air, but they did not
do, and had to return to their glass. A
lovely face gazes at me all the time I write,
and will not suffer itself to be neglected!
It is a choice white Cactus of great size,
with warm lemon colouring in the outer

leaves. The stamens are so delicately set, they tremble at the slightest touch, and the starry pointal is itself a flower !

JUNE.

A Mosaic of Nectared Sweets.

IX.

JUNE.

Of Pink May—Swallows in the Porch—Flowers de Luce
—Poppies—A Little Scotch Rose, and "Clutie."

June 6.—It is difficult to know what to say
about the garden in June.   There is so much
to say, I can hardly tell how to begin.   The
leafy month earns well its title, so grandly
full-leafed are the trees; in finer leaf, I think,
than they have been for many a year.   The
Elms stand out against the sky in rounded
blocks of green, and in the Lime avenue the
broad leaves meeting overhead are round
and pure in outline, untouched as yet by
destroying worms, untorn by tempests.   The
young Horse Chestnuts along the little watercourse are nearly twice the size they were

last summer, when cruel winds had left them
only a few ragged discoloured leaves. The
flower-spikes of a Chestnut within the garden
measure near a foot in length. The great
red Horse Chestnut (*Pavias rubra*) is red all
over; it is a mass of blossom almost from the
ground upwards to the very top. The tree
is a fine sight, and if it were not so common
one scarcely should tire of admiring it. The
season makes a great difference in the colouring of the blossoms. Sometimes they come
out almost yellow, from too little sun and too
much rain; but in the rich *floraison* of to-day
their colour is almost crimson. Then the
Thorns are in great perfection; the branches
of double Pink May can be compared to
nothing else but bars of pink velvet. The
double scarlet varieties are finer than
usual, and under the hot sun their vivid
colour is quite dazzling. We find this sort
rather capricious; some years there is
more green than red, and when the trees
were younger the red was finer. A little
single Thorn draped itself down to the very
grass in scarlet bloom; but it lasts so brief
a time that every petal now has fallen. It is a

picturesque, delightful tendency in all trees
to bend and stretch out to meet each other;
their branches love to touch and interlace.
So, at this time, across many of our green garden walks the flowering May makes beautiful
red-garlanded arches.   Pink May and Laburnum interweave their branches, and in
another place a Cherry and a Thorn have
succeeded in meeting.   A little further on,
an Apple reaches out long arms above the
turf to touch a copper Beech.   Here, in this
corner, there is also Laurel; and Brake
Fern, springing of itself, will soon be tall
enough to reach almost the Apple branches.
The Beeches, on either side the *Allée Verte*,
embower the walk, while along the outmost
line their slender drooping shoots stretch
themselves to meet and embrace more staid
and slow young Elm branchlets, spreading
from the great old trees.   The nightingale's
old White Thorn shone white like a great
snow mountain for about ten days, surpassing all the rest in beauty; and not far from
it, deep in a thorny thicket of Dewberry
mixed with Ivy and Nettles, we found the
nightingale's nest.   I often visited her, and

she would lie close, with head laid back, and
bright, black, watchful eye fixed full upon
me ; but I never saw **her** strange, smoked
eggs, because she would never stir from the
nest. Massive gleams—if such an anomaly
can be said—of yellow Spanish and English
Broom are shining between green trees, in
contrast with paler gold of overhanging
Laburnum. I wonder if the Riviera Broom
would live in this **climate.** I mean the
Broom that grows something like a Rush,
with the flowers set all round its polished
stem.* In the orchard border an immense
luxuriantly rounded bush of Weigela **re-**
places the Pyrus of last month, the lovely
pink of its blossom set **off by** the tender
green around it. These are **all** beautiful
bits of colour, and yet they are only
samples, as it were, of what I wish and
may partly hope for some day ; for a
Laburnum colonnade is in contemplation,
and lilac closes, and golden cloisters of
Genista, some day, there must be ! Something also should be made of the pale hang-

---

* *Spartium junceum.*

ing clusters of Wistaria—a *pergola* ceiled
in with its lilac pendants, or small bushes
standing alone, in some grassy place. Our
Rhododendrons and Azaleas are in great
beauty, and since last year, are grown and
filled out; the season seems in some way to
have pleased them well. We do not attempt
fine sorts, though there is just a sprinkling
of crimson and white and a few others,
amongst the showy old pinkish-lilac sort.
The broad border by the side of the
walk along the Holly hedge is filled with
Rhododendrons and Azaleas; as yet only
the common—yet always beautiful—yellow
and creamy-white Azalea, filling all the air
with its peculiar scent. The success of this
border is especially pleasant, for the young
Americans made one rather nervous at times
during the early spring—on days when the
weather did not exactly suit them they would
look so pitiable and dejected, with their
leaves hanging straight down. Into this
border were moved most of the aged drawn-
up Rhododendrons, that used to crowd the
shrubberies. Here, with more room, they
have begun to bush out healthily. Yet there

is at present no peat or made-up bed, and the ground is flooded every winter. We think of giving them a few cartloads of peat next autumn, just by way of encouragement. In another year this walk will deserve to be called "the Rhododendron Walk." At the back of the border two double scarlet May trees are now radiant with blossom. About three years ago they were removed here out of the garden, where for some reason they had become sickly and had ceased to bloom. Change of air and scene has worked wonders: they have increased greatly in size, and the move is apparently forgotten. Beyond these is the new orchard, deep in growing grass, and then the Larch Walk; and— and then—palings, if the truth must out! Beyond the Holly hedge, in the shrubbery, wherein we stuff everything that has nowhere else to go, there is at this moment a white glory of snow-balled Gueldres Rose. In my ideal garden there shall be large single trees of Gueldres Rose standing alone; not, as they generally are grown, "smored up" with crowded shrubs.

But we have wandered far away from the

beloved garden. Over the south porch is the Lady's Bower—the chamber always so called in old English houses—with Vine-wreathed windows. Swallows are building in the garden porch. It is the chimney swallow, with the red throat. Their confidence and tameness, the perpetual darting in and out of blue-black wings (like tenderly domesticated trout! as Mr. Ruskin says), and the conversational cheery twitter that goes on all day long, are a continual feast. South, north, and east are the three porches of the house, and swallows in all three. At the north they are more bold, but somehow less familiar. Darting shoals of swallows dash in and out, through the open doors into the house, and two nests are now nearly built. The family motto, " God's providence is my inheritance," written round the porch walls, suits well such a place of birds ; while the footless martin—sign of the seventh son—borne on the stone shield over the door among the Roses and Ivy, our swallows may also feel to be not wholly inappropriate. Under the east porch, which is now green with Virginian Creeper and Vine—and which

10

will be in its season purple with Clematis, a pair of swallows are arranging a settlement. Here also, though not quite so welcome, no one dreams of denying them. After the sun has turned the corner of the house, this porch is cool and shady. On the threshold is set the legend, " Nos et meditemur in horto," taken from a sun-dial in the nuns' garden at Polesworth, near Tamworth. The invitation, I think, is generally disregarded. Many cross that threshold to walk in the garden and admire the flowers, or to play tennis, or perhaps—to smoke. But I do not think people often meditate much in the garden in these days. Dogs do sometimes, as they sit in the sun. But I wonder how it is done !

From the south front a lot of Everlasting Pea has wound itself round between the wall and the Yew buttress, taking up fully one half of the porch. It is well named Everlasting ! One has nothing to do but to dig it up, and cut and hack it away, and the next year it will appear strong and hearty and in double quantity. It takes no hint that there may be too much of a good thing ! And yet, when it looks so fresh and hand-

some, with its large bright flowers, it would
be cruel to wish it away. So let it be, to
teach its lesson and to smother as it will.
The white Irises are nearly over, and Wood
Strawberries begin to redden under the
windows. An old Maiden's Blush Rose,
covered with buds, peeps in at the dining-
room window on one side, and on the
other is the lovely pink of a most perfect
Moss Rose. The parterr in front of the
window is bedded out, of course. I know
that it soon will be a blaze of well-chosen
colour; but excepting the golden mount of
Stonecrop in the centre, I do not take much
personal interest in its summer phase. It
is fortunate for the garden's character that
this should be so; for as the invention of
new combinations of plants and colours would
be to me impossible, this is left always in
our Gardener's hands, with full confidence
that the result will be as perfect as such
things can be. From the dining-room window we can also see, between the Sumac
and a Box tree, near where a Pæony showers
crimson on the daisies, a tiny mound of turf.
It has been there since the end of last month;

and under it lies the dear little favourite
of nine summers—Clutie, the little black
Skye terrier. She always loved the dining-
room! . . . We can now almost walk all
round the garden in deep cool shade, such
growth the trees have made! The Broad
Walk must always be exposed to the sun;
but from the west of it, across the lawn where
the old bowling-green once was, the distance
from shade to shade lessens year by year
as the trees grow on. There is a charming
well-shaded welt along the grass, of purple
Pansies and white Pinks, in two thick lines;
and on the sunny side a very bright dash of
Limnanthes Douglasii has made a self-sown
edging. As if it enjoyed the pleasant cool-
ness of a north-west border, one lovely
double Narcissus still lingers on in her
early freshness. When hot sunbeams
pierce the shade, every day I think must
be her last. The Spurge Laurel has re-
lapsed into the plain dulness of its summer
state, but the Iris bank upon which it grows
is as lovely as heart can desire. Cedar and
Copper Beech and one or two Firs cast light
shadows upon the company of Irises, and help

them not to wither up too quickly. The pre-
vailing hue is lilac, with stronger tones, and
yellows intermixed. Each one in turn seems
loveliest, but one chief beauty (*Iris pallida*)
has broad petals of soft grey, most delicately
flushed with pink. Then there are lilacs
marked with deeper lines and white with
lilac edges (*Iris aphylla*), finely pencilled;
Enchantress, and several other yellow
Variegatas, with lines of red or brown;
pale yellow, with the three outer petals
intense velvety-purple; and one pale bluish,
with deep blue-purple velvet outside, and
bright yellow brush, well marked. These
two are much better than gay Darius, or the
handsome sullen Versailles. The sober old
Marquise (*Iris lurida*), too—who is, however, more like Mrs. Delany in dove-coloured
mode silk hood!—after long delay, is there
amongst the best. Does any plant exist that
loves not a corner or an edge? I think not
one; so a little corner here, where a narrow
grass path crosses the Iris bank into the
Beechen close, is made especially lovely by
the undesigned grouping of three Irises, enriched by a background of green Ferns and

Beech. The centre of the group is a deep red-purple Iris (from Vesuvius), a finely coloured yellow and purple, and between them a pure white. These grow tall and stately from out their straight stiff leaves, while a little Welsh Poppy, established there by chance, brings in its crumpled lemon-gold with the happiest effect. Colour effects, wherever they appear in our garden, are seldom planned. Somehow it does not come naturally to think, "Here there shall be blue Larkspur and white Lilies," or there red Poppies and something else. But it is quite an exquisite delight to find the most beautiful accidents of colour in unexpected places all about the garden. Then these chances may give hints, which we can take or not. At a corner behind the dovecote there is a grand crimson Pæony, mixed up with brilliant orange Marigolds, some of them black-eyed; red and yellow are splendid, if well used. Against the dark brown of a Cryptomeria Elegans stands a tall Tulip, like white china painted and streaked blood-red; at least it is over now, but I see it all the same. Then there is a patch of Welsh

Poppy, growing just as one finds a patch
of Gentian or white Crocus on the Alps—
and with it London Pride, a mass of feathery
red, growing in the same way. Under the
trees, one meets a pallid Columbine, looking
like a ghost, and just by chance in the lilac
Iris bed occurs one rich carmine Rose.
I do not even think the delicately refined
colour combination of dwarf-growing Gloire
de Dijon Roses and bronze Heartsease
was quite intentional ; they mix, however,
strangely well. And the bed of pink Roses
—Prevost and Jules Margottin—with the
white Pink " Mrs. Sinkins," promises to be
an equal success.

One would fain stay for awhile the steps
of the summer flowers in the garden ; but
these bright daughters of the year, in long
procession, flit by more swiftly as each new
day arises. They are in such a hurry now
to come and to be gone, alas ! Even at this
very moment there are signs of the quick
approach of some of our latest loves. For
in the east border, among crimson Pæonies
and lingering purple Iris, appears already
a single Dahlia ! In such a multitude one

hardly knows which flowers to note, they are all so fair. But in the Fantaisie, I think I could almost let the Roses go which are bursting into bloom as bushes and as pillar Roses, just to keep it a little longer as it is now, with the hosts of White Foxgloves, with double white Rockets, yellow Day Lilies, and puce-purple Columbines; Irises and white stars of Nicotiana rising over an edging of pink and white Phlox Nelsoni—all these and many more, set off by Cupressus and Fir, interspersed among the flowers beyond; and flaring across the grass walk, a great fiery scarlet Oriental Poppy. With the morning shining through it, this flower seems made up of fire from the sun itself—the very purest possible essence of scarlet. Several magnificent Poppies light up the garden at different points. Their scarlet is a fast colour; neither wind nor sun will scorch or change it in the least, and in this quality it is superior to so many flowers whose colours fly directly—some more easily than others. The brown Hearts-ease cannot stand the sun, while the large purple is unmoved. The crimson of the

Pæony flies; and the rose-red double Pyrethrum scorches quickly. Lilac (excepting in Wistaria) seems one of the fastest colours in the garden!—though rain-drops standing all night in a half-faded lilac Iris become a most beautiful colour! Although it seems that scarlet, yellows, and colours in which blue is mixed stand best. Besides the great scarlet Poppies, the annual Poppies are coming on, in all their varied pinks, and reds, and whites; their large crumpled petals have the shape and all the transparent delicacy of rare sea shells. There is also a charming uncertainty as to the colours or amount of doubleness to be expected. Amongst the best are bright reds with a clear white eye, and pink-hemmed whites. But whenever anything approaching a common field Poppy makes its appearance amongst them—as often happens, they have such a strong tendency to run back—it has to be pulled up immediately. Our Columbines are not so fine as they were last summer; their flowers are smaller and not so free in form. The Californian scarlet and yellow is so small as to be a miniature of itself. There is, however, one fine plant with flowers pale violet and primrose, and the various tints of "crushed strawberry" are very lovely, especially in the double Columbines.

June 15.—Here is the middle of the month, and the garden is more bewildering than ever! Rosebuds in countless multitudes are blooming everywhere, in every part. And as the fashion is to call her so, we must allow the Rose to be queen of flowers; and since it is most true that Roses are—

" Not royal in their smells alone, but in their hue,"

so, though my beloved Iris has not yet faded from the garden, the Rose now must be worshipped. One by one we have already greeted many of our old best favourites. Amongst them Boursault came first, climbing the south gables of the house; then Souvenir d'un Ami, large and full flushed, at the very top of the long bare old stem of a climber, any age; then Gloire de Dijon, which, though even more profuse in its bloom than usual, has a something not quite right about it this year—a sort of old expression. After that, Maiden's Blush and Moss Rose. A great wild blush of Boursault Rose grows

at the north end of the garden—the flowers
are lovely, recalling a little in their colour
and irregular shape what I remember as
" the Musk Rose," in the gardens of former days. Coupe d'Hébé, on the wall of
the gardener's cottage, is perfect in scent
and shape and in true rose-colour. The
yellow Briar is finer than usual, and Damask
Roses are opening fast. La France, too—
the Rose whose scent is made of the finest
attar—has delighted us with half-a-dozen
beautiful blooms; Blairii No. 2 begins to
crest the wire arches (one never hears of No.
1 !). But among the Rose joys which abound
already, or that we still expect in endless
succession, none are so dear to me as one
little ragged bush, covered now with small
white Scotch Roses of exquisite perfume.
This little Rose bush is forty-eight years old,
to my certain knowledge. It was planted by
my father, and it has been mine for the last
twenty years. Last year it showed some
signs of feebleness, so we moved it from the
over-crowded place where it had been for
eleven years, into a newly made bed with a
south aspect. There, with a companion of

the same kind, it promises to take a new lease of life. Strange that such a little Rose should thus live on for well-nigh half a century, calmly putting forth its leaf and bloom summer after summer, whilst so many of the men and women who knew it once have passed away! It somehow makes one think of the old monk pointing to the frescoes on his convent walls, and saying, "These are the realities; we are the shadows."

A word of praise must be said for the blue and green of Anchusa Italica at the southern end of the Broad Walk, and the beds of white Pinks (these are the old-fashioned "maiden pinks of odour faint"), mixing their perfume deliciously with Musk. The beds and large patches of beautiful "Mrs. Sinkins" are very good this season. They are, as Bacon would say, "fast flowers of their smell," in flavour like Clove Carnations.

JULY.

" As the last taste of sweet is sweetest last,
Writ in remembrance more than things
long past."—SHAKESPEARE.

X.

MIDSUMMER AND JULY.

Of Pæonies—Iris Sibirica—Green Peas—Fennel—Strawberries—Lilies—The Vine.

June 24.—"Ere the parting hour go by, quick,
thy tablets, Memory." In less than a week
July will be here, and June will fade away
into the past and be forgotten, while more
than half its loveliness is still unnoted and
untold. So here on Midsummer night, when
the spirits of earth and air have power, let
me call back for a moment the dear-worth
vision of flowers that were my delight in
the gone sweet days of early June. I would
try also to fix the remembrance of a few,
out of the thousand glories of the day,
doomed to die before ever the story of next

month begins. And first the Pæonies, which I have as yet scarcely named. Earliest of all came the crimson-pink single Pæony (*Pæonia peregrina*), with yellow stamens and bluish leaves, like a giant Rose of Sharon (the single red Scotch Rose); then the pale pink double; then the heavy crimson, that pales so quick in sun or rain; then, most beautiful of all, the pure, cold, white Pæony, with a faint tinge of colour on its outer petals. Last of all the large rose-red—rose-coloured, with an evanescent perfume like a dream of the smell of a wild Rose, yet in substance so staunch a flower that I have known rose Pæonies retain their beauty for two full weeks in a glass of water. All these, excepting one or two who here and there outstay the rest, are gone by.

And then the Elder! The hedgerows have been white with it; and there were days when all the air was scented with it, and the country smelt of Elder! The path under our one tree is now a milky way, covered with a myriad little fallen stars. They remind one of the far-away Olives'

starry blossoms, when they fall softly among
Lady Tulips and Gladioli in May. Syringa
(*Philadelphus*, or Mock Orange) has come and
almost gone ; three varieties—the old small
one, the large-flowered, and the half-double
sort. I like most the first, and this has also
the most powerful scent. A large old bush
of it grows in the grass, just without the glass
door in the wall opening into the greenhouse. Dear Syringa ! best hated and best
loved of flowers. The lovers of it hail its
blooming with enthusiasm, and break off
sprigs to wear as they pass the bush, whilst
others will go the other way round to avoid
passing near. And now it suffers still further
insult by being denied its own old name,
Syringa ! Even in 1597, in Gerarde's time,
there began to arise some confusion between it and the Lilac, or " Blew Pipe Tree."

And now, at this very time, has come
a new burst of Irises—the narrow-leaved
kinds. Not the real Spanish Irises; their
time is not yet. We have a few old plants
whose flowers are deep bronze, flame-
centred, in yellow gold, and a stronger,
commoner kind, of full lilac colour. One

little plant, growing in a pet corner by the
iron gate in the south wall, has a delicate
primrose and lilac-tipped bloom. And there
is the great white Flag Iris, whose grand
leaves stand four feet high. The right
place has not yet been found for this fine
plant. For three years past he has just
borne with us, and no more; I fear he
dislikes us—and he shows it. By the
watercourse the yellow Flags are as yellow
as possible, in rich contrast with their
dark green leaves; and in the Fantaisie,
where the China Tulip stood last month,
showing bright against the dusky Cryptomeria Elegans, is now a fine root of Iris
(*Sibirica alba*). The blue Sibirica is good,
but this white variety is most lovely. One
could not pass it by without remarking the
peculiar whiteness **of** its small shapely
flowers, set on such long slender stalks.
How wonderful are the contrasts of white in
flowers! Of those now in bloom together,
one hardly knows which to call the whitest
of them all. This little Iris retains through
its whiteness a dim remembrance, as it were,
of blue.

There is the kitchen garden, too! The
fresh and brilliant beauty that just now
it holds within its walls will soon be past,
giving place to richer, more sober colours.
Looking through the old ironwork of the
gate, up the straight middle walk, there is
such a splendour of brightly blended colour
in the flowers on either side! As yet, they
are in their prime; the key-note of colour
is white—double Rockets, double white
Pyrethrums, and white Pinks. Then, bending down over the walk, mixing in with
the whiteness, glowing through leaf and
branch in brilliant intervals of colour, are
Roses—pink, crimson, blush; Annual Poppies, tender or dazzling in their hue; clouds
of pale blue Delphinium, with spires of
deepening blue over-topping all the rest.
Just midway between the pink and crimson
Roses, a Briar, wreathed about with small
yellow blooms, hangs over the cross walks
at the corner. Masses of low blue Campanula fill in below or between the larger
flowers. Right at the end, another iron
gate lets in the glimmering of cool shades
beyond. A little wren's nest is there,

ensconced snugly in a bowery Clematis, half-way up the pillar; the nest cannot be seen so far off, but I know well how the small entrance hole is quite filled up with greedy little yellow beaks and gaping mouths! The little mother is hard at work for them, somewhere near—hunting the bark of an Elm, most likely. The golden wrens have brought out their families—two nestfuls. We found the nests hanging in the Yews, and now the garden seems to be full of little elfin scissors' grinders, busy all day long.

I have a fancy to open the gate and go all round the kitchen garden quite prosaically. The other garden will seem still sweeter, after. Here, on the left, is a breadth of wonderful Lettuces, round and close like small round Cabbages, with milk-white middles; and beyond, some taller and tied-up—more like Salad. Near the Lettuces are tall ranks of Peas, hung all over with well-filled pods. I think I like these beautiful green Peas, growing here, as much as when served up in a dish for dinner. There seems always to be something attractive to

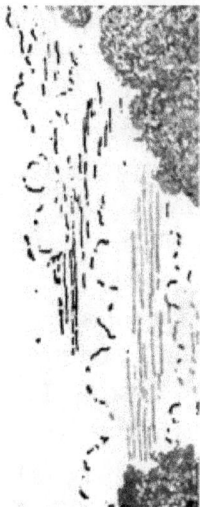

Art of all kinds in pea pods; from the pods sculptured on the great bronze gates of the cathedral at Pisa, or the raised needlework of the sixteenth century, to the ornaments in the jewellers' shops of Paris or the portraits of Marrowfats or Telegraph Peas in the advertisement-sheets of gardening papers—these last being really pictures, though not meant so. I remember once being shown a white satin spencer of Queen Elizabeth's, embroidered in butterflies and Green Pea pods half-open, to show the rows of peas within.

I think there is Beetroot, and a fine lot of young Cabbages, beyond the Peas—in which no one can feel any particular interest; and oh! such a sweet patch of seedling Mrs. Sinkins white Pink. I wish that Pink did possess a more poetical name—Arethusa or Boule de Neige! but the thing is done, and to the end of time Mrs. Sinkins will be herself. Next comes a little square of Japanese Iris, the tall stems tipped with swelling buds whose grand unfolding I long to see. Rows of young Sage plants grow near, quite unlike sage-green, so-called, in

colour; and a nice little plantation of healthy-
looking Fennel. That is for broiled mackerel;
but there is to me another interest connected
with Fennel, that lies in a lurking hope,
always unfulfilled, of finding upon it a
caterpillar of the rare *Papilio regina.*
Caterpillars of another sort are only too
multitudinous on the Currants growing
up the walls. The increase of them, and
of the sawflies belonging to them, is not
short of miraculous. One may stamp out
whole families and clear the bushes, and
next morning they will be beginning again.
Yet invariably in the act of destroying
there creeps in a sort of questioning, whether
the caterpillars have not full as good a right
to the Currants as we have—except, indeed,
that we, and not they, planted them. But
the sawflies would seem to have at least a
right to live—a greater right, perhaps, than
we to have tarts; yet they are spared none the
more for such-like uncomfortable reflections.
On the south wall the fruit trees seem to be
more or less flourishing. An old Nectarine
is covered with fruit. Then comes Apricot
tree No. 1, on which I find no Apricots;

Nos. 2 and **3 the same,** 4 dead, and 5 with
" a good few" on it. Then we come to
Peaches, plenty of them; then a beautiful dark-leafed Fig tree; and then the
Cherries, well fruited and well netted. And
so on round the walls. Near the wren's
nest there is another large patch of Pinks,
commoner and better than any, with the
neatest lacing of purple-madder or lake.
And here a powerful fragrance stops one
short; it is the strawberries, smelling deliciously. They are littered down with clean
straw, and netted close, for the discomfiture
of blackbirds. The scent takes me back a
very long way—back to an inconceivable
time, when this old smell of Strawberries,
borne across the hedge in the hot noontide
of some summer holiday, was reason enough
to set us wild vagrants of the garden
scrambling through the thorns to seize the
exquisite delight of spoiling our neighbour's
Strawberries—a joy that was never marred,
for we were never found out. Sun and rain
have both been kind, and this **is** our second
week of immense red Presidents, one of
the oldest and best of strawberries—the

older Caroline being now quite forgotten. The espaliers are showing plenty of Apples and Pears. Three Pear trees, standing at the four cross-ways, are curiously in bloom; the blossoms are all sickly-looking and undersized, but the trees are covered with them up to the very top, while fruit is set at the same time. I dislike this unnatural blooming, for the mind will persist in reverting to foolish sayings and superstitions connected with trees bearing fruit and flower at the same time.

Among the pleasant sights of this midsummertide, perhaps the pleasantest of all is the great thicket of wild Roses growing within the wire network that bounds the tennis-lawn on the garden side. The east, shining full upon it every morning, brings forth hundreds of new-blown Roses. Very often, as you pass into their sweet presence from under the Plane trees, the air is redolent of a subtle perfume—not always, though, nor every day, for Roses are capricious of their scent. The yellow-stamened centre of each flower glows like a tiny lamp of gold, and the soft petals surrounding it are rose-pink of

the tenderest dye. Were these the canker-
blooms of Shakespeare? If so, and if in
his day they could be said to " live unwooed,
and unrespected die," surely now the tide
has turned, for the wild Rose is beloved of
all ; while we must confess that garden Roses
now-a-days do not always " die sweet
deaths."

July 22.—

  " It is not growing like a tree
   In bulk that makes man better be.
    The Lily of a day
    Is fairer far in May :
   Although it fall and die that night,
   It was the plant and flower of light."

        Ben Jonson.

Once more our favourite old Ben! Roses
are gone, and the memory of them is as
of something too beautiful for words. And
Lilies, too, are over; the fairest of them,
the tall white Lily, with her shining head
—*nil candidius*—pure as the shining robe
of saints in heaven—better than Solomon
in his glory. She, too, is past; nothing of
her remains but long dismal stems, with
down-hanging shrivelled leaves and melan-

East Gate.

choly pointals undrest of beauty—to tell of
her former pride.

The character and features of the Lily
would seem to be well marked enough;
and yet, sometimes, the popular idea of it
is certainly a mixed one. In former days
flower-hawkers in the streets of London may
be remembered crying, "Lilies, fine white
Lilies!" with their barrow-loads of white
Thorn, or May blossom, from the country.
Some botanical reason there must have been
for the Lilies in Ferrari's " De Florum Cul-
tura" (1633) being named Narcissus! I have
been studying an odd volume of this curious
old book, and the unmistakable Lilies
represented in the plates are all "Narcissus Indicus." Even the Water-lily-like
Blood Flower is a Narcissus. Very likely
these remarks may only show my ignorance.

July must be all retrospect, for all is over
—or so it seems to me. After an absence
of a few days, on returning to the garden, I
find there is a change—an almost autumnal
feeling in the air, and withered leaves are
blown across the lawn. Faint perfumes
linger still about the Limes, and though

no song birds are there, the sound of bees
is heard in the green depths above. But
we no longer would breakfast under the
Limes, as we did so short a while since, in
summer days departed. Wind and rain have
done their worst amongst the flowers, and
yet there is consolation in all that remains.
The best are passed away, but beautiful
new things are coming on. The Evening
Primrose (*Ænothera*) already lights up the
garden ways. Variegated Maples, with their
foliage white as ivory, look their best against
the darkening Elms.* The hedge of Sweet
Peas is for the moment in beauty. Sweet
Peas go off too quickly in our light warm
soil, so we try to prolong their blooming to
the latest limit by cutting off their pods as
fast as they appear.

Purple draperies of Clematis (Virgin's
Bower), in many shades, from the deepest
violet softening into grey, make the old brick
walls beautiful ; or the same Clematis droops

---

* A small branchlet in one of these white Maples
has returned to the original green, and this is also
the sole bit of the tree that bears a *bunch of keys*.

from trellises, or clambers up the trees in
many parts of the garden.   Almost always it
so happens that the tender green of Vines
mingles with the purple.   There is something almost unpleasing in the arrangement
of the four petals of Clematis Jackmanni!
but much must be forgiven for the sake of
such grand colouring.   No climbing plant
comes near the Vine, perhaps, in perfect grace
and beauty of line.   The fruitful Vine gives
delight to the eye in far larger measure than
Virginia Creeper, or any other of our green
hangings upon the walls of a house.   The
Vine is more obedient and yet more free,
and its intelligence is greater.   Thinking of
the Vine as of a person, one would say that
her foliage shows all the variety of genius.
Scarcely will you find two leaves alike, in
shape, or size, or colour.   The youngest
leaves are half-transparent and golden-green,
or reddened by the sun ; on some the light
lies cold and grey.   If the Vine is trained
round the window, the leaves seen from
within outspread against the light glow
like green fires.   The very shadiest recesses
of the Vine are full of light.   And then the

tenderness and strength of her slender beautiful tendrils! How they reach out like
sentient hands! and when they have found,
how strong and firm their clasp! Then,
who does not know and love the curious
aroma of her small green flowers, bringing
back to memory the smell of a Southern
vineyard? Very soon, now, autumn suns
will swell the clustered fruit, and purple
bloom will begin to show between the leaves.
A Vine is one of the only plants whose every
leaf, well nigh, may be painted with care in
a picture, and yet not seem too much made
out. Yet rarely indeed can human hand
give the fine thinness and yielding texture
of a Vine leaf!

We are never without Portulaca and
Mesembryanthemum (how far more simple
is the old name—Fig Marigold) about this
time, and the two beds of them now flowering are especially brilliant. Cool colours
tell beside the scarlet and orange that mostly
prevail, and in this way nothing could be
more refreshing than the dwarf Ageratum
and blue Lobelia, mixed with honey-scented
Koniga Maritima Variegata, near the Carna-

tions and Portulaca. The deep blue, with bronze foliage, of the Lobelia beds in the parterr is almost hot beside the cooler blues beyond. The Sumac this year is not in beauty—not as if a sunset cloud had settled down upon it. The multitude of new green shoots would seem to overpower the crimsoned fluff.

AUGUST.

12

The Garden is a mute Gospel.
The Garden is a perpetual Gala.

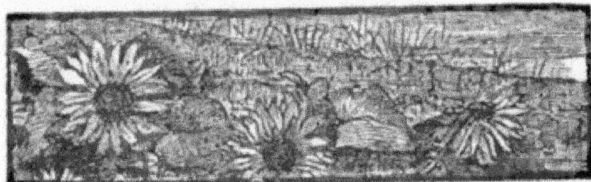

XI.

AUGUST.

"My Sunflower"—Of a Garden Sunday—Of Ghosts in
the Twilight—Magnolia Grandiflora.

August 6.—The Lime avenue is pleasanter
than ever now, on these bright afternoons
when the low sun strikes amber shafts
through the branches, and light shadows lie
on the parquet of brown and yellow leaves
beneath. With every breeze hundreds of
the winged sea-vessels, like queer little
teetotums, come twirling down. The wrens
are busy with their second or third nests—
without counting the cock-nests at the beginning of the season ; the porch swallows are
thinking of a second brood, and scatter straws
of hay and patches of wet mud untidily upon

the stones underneath their nests; thrushes
go about the lawn followed by two or three
great awkward young ones (their third family
this season), too foolish to pick up worms
for themselves. As for the sparrows, they
are hard at work with probably the sixth or
seventh nest of their series. Roses are coming
on in their second bloom; low bushes and
standards of La France show large buds and
attar-scented blossoms; while crimson Roses
of many names glow in richest bloom here
and there all over the garden. Precious as
are these late Roses, the chord of colour has
changed so much since Roses were in their
prime, that fresh pink or crimson seem
almost misplaced among the fiery reds and
scarlet. White Roses are seldom so beautiful as one feels they ought to be; but a
small plant of the Japanese Rosa Rugosa, in
its first season with us, has been a great pet
this summer, with its large white petals; the
Macartney also is welcome, flowering as it
has for the first time in its life here. The
buds have hitherto always fallen off, without
an attempt at unclosing, and it has only kept
its place on the wall for the sake of the

lovely evergreen leaves and yearly promise
of abundant bloom. But the only perfect
white Rose, the White Moss, remains still
for me a dream and nothing more. There
are tall old bluish-pink Roses at the back
of the Beechen close which have been
blooming in almost rank luxuriance. They,
with a few Cabbage Roses and Maiden's
Blush, and a yellow Banksia, were all of
Roses the garden had when first we came
here, eleven years ago. At that time they
were thought too ugly almost to live, and
were banished to the outskirts. But time
has brought them round to the front again ;
and now these relics of a bygone Rose age
are beloved for their redundant and perfumed bloom, and for their most uncommon
colour, the red in them being so largely mixed
with cold blue. The York and Lancaster
Rose—long lost and long coveted—will, I
hope, ere next season be established with
us. For the other day in Somersetshire we
found one growing near a ghostly house in
a deserted garden, and from this plant we
have some healthy suckers. I cannot keep
pace with the new Roses ; they are mostly

too large and heavy. They seem to run too far from the flatness of a really typical Rose type.

We have not made *pot pourri* this summer; but the Lavender harvest is gathered in, with spikes unusually fine. I am not sure that they smell much the sweeter for their great size. It is a pleasant time when the Lavender is laid out in trays, and the house is full of the sweetness of it. On these bright windy mornings the Broad Walk looks its best. Looking up from south to north, the end of the walk, framed in with trees, is bounded by a low Quickset hedge, beyond which lies meadow-land, with glimpses of yellow corn-fields. Beyond all is the soft blue of distant wood. Along the Yew hedge, on one side, are long borders in the turf of single Dahlias, in succession to Sweet-williams (Bearded pink); and the other side under the wall is enriched with scarlet, the scarlet of those tall Lychnis which the children call "Summer Lightning" (*Lychnis chalcedonia*, flower of Bristow and Constantinople). And there are sheaves of finely dyed rose-red Phloxes, pyramids of blue and white Campanula, and clumps of dark blue Salvia; grey and feathery Gypsophila Paniculata also—priceless for the setting off of delicate Poppies and other refined and frail kinds when cut. Yet the mass of colour would be far more brilliant but for the bulbs which lie hidden under the earth. They must not be disturbed by planting in amongst them, so all that is in the border has its place there perennially.

Spaces in the wall behind—where the ancient Pear trees may have perished from old age—are sometimes dressed in spreading Vines. Last month a tall blue Larkspur, near one of these Vines, was caught by the wandering tendrils, and so they grew together, the Larkspur upheld by her friend the Vine with a strong and tender grasp. Green streamers of this Vine also wreathe the head of an iron gate empurpled with intermingling Clematis. Here also, close to the old wall, at regular intervals, are our Sunflowers; some of them grow to nearly ten feet in height. After many trials of other spots, we think they seem to do best planted thus. The shelter saves them

all conflict with wind and rain, and they
are tall, and straight, and full, having no
cares of weather to divert their gradual
growth to beauty.   There was a time when
I did not love Sunflowers.   Their constant
repetition as a kind of æsthetic badge can
scarcely fail to tire.   In those days they
had no place in the garden, or only in some
out-of-the-way obscure corner.   But once
I found a little song of William Blake's, and
ever since, for the music of it, the Sunflower
has been beloved, with the feeling that to
know her is to give her your heart.

> " Ah, Sunflower ! weary of time,
>   Who countest the steps of the sun,
>   Seeking after that sweet golden prime
>   Where the traveller's journey is done,
>   Where the youth pined away with desire,
>   And the pale virgin, shrouded in snow,
>   Arise from their graves and aspire
>   Where my Sunflower wishes to go."

Perhaps there is not much of common sense
in the words ! but they surely are most
musical.   How grand these Sunflowers are !
and there is a sweet and gracious look in the
Sunflower's open face.   With all her grand

mien and stately stature, she never stares up
direct at her god; the golden head half
bends down; downward also point the
symmetrically set broad leaves, delicately
shaped *en cœur.* The whole aspect is one
of contemplation, or at least one fancies it
to be so. There is also a sort of majesty in
the one strong single stem, from which pro-
ceeds so fine a show of buds, and flowers,
and leaves. Yet I have never been happy
enough to see her act the part of the poet's
Sunflower—the real Sunflower of our earthly
gardens could never turn her head so fast;
all that I know she does is to bloom on
whichever side of her the sun rises. Poets,
nevertheless, are the true seers, and without doubt they know what they say. The
French name, "Tournesol," would seem to
imply a popular belief that the flower
follows the sun.

The silly Dahlia would turn her face to
the wall or any way. Brilliant as are these
single Dahlias, they are rather trying in their
ways; so much rank leaf and stalk, and so
little flower; the plants sometimes too
large and bushy, sometimes too thin; and

then it is so irritating when their backs are
turned as one passes along the walk! The
so-called Cactus Dahlia is not at all tire-
some; it is beautiful both in form and
colour.

Aug. 26.   *Sunday Morning.*—After a hundred years, if the Seven Sleepers awoke on
an English Sunday morning, they would
certainly at once know what day it was.
There is nothing else like it for the feeling
of intense repose.   No other stillness can
compare with the deep calm of a Sunday
morning such as this.   No leaf stirs; there
is no cloud moving about in the hot hazy
blue; the clatter of the iron road has ceased;
the very birds are still.   Swallows alone are
ever on the wing, and the silence is so
profound that the beat of their wings can be
heard as they dart by in rapid course.   The
busy corn-fields lie empty in a golden rest.
Only here and there, where the harvest is
not yet gathered in, the sheaves, like praying
hands, stand together on the field.   In the
green pastures the grazing cattle seem to
tread with hushed and silent step.   And

there is a sound of church bells on the air,
coming clear yet faint across the level
country. There will be no church for the
tired harvestmen whom we saw yesterday
lying on the dusty grass by the roadside.
They are too tired, and too ragged and dirty;
but we may hope for them also some rest-
ful influences from the quiet of the day,
under such a blue sky.

The early morning is always the time of
all others for the garden, while the flowers
are refreshed with the dew and darkness
and cool of night, and are rejoicing yet in
the light of a new sun. Soon they will
begin to flag in the dry weary round of
burning hours. To one who only knows
the garden after 8 o'clock a.m., a walk
round it between 7 or 8, or earlier, would
be a revelation. On this special morning the
flowers in the east border seem penetrated
through and through with the rapture of
existence. Each Sunflower stands with half-
transparent shadow sharp cut upon the wall
behind it, its petals fresh gilt, its centre
sparkling with dew; rose-red Phlox and
flaming Sword Lilies (Corn-flag), blue Salvia

intermixed with many-coloured stars of Dahlias, and an indescribable mob of smaller,
more insignificant things. Round the corner
a great mass of common white Clematis fills
the air with fragrance. It is all whiteness and
sweetness; it is a summer cloud, a white
cumulus of surpassing beauty. One of the
stone vases of the gate pillars is completely
hidden under the white foam. But this
matters not; nothing matters but that we
should have the Clematis there, in its loveliness! The Tigridias in the entrance court
are wide open, and none would guess how
brief their hours were to be. There are a few
perfect Roses—morning glories (*Convolvulus major*), and orange Tropœolums ("Lark-
heels trim") with bluish leaves. The dew
lies upon all, and one may say in the garden
the Psalmist's words about the valleys thick
with corn, for the flowers all seem to laugh
and sing with joy. Ten glorious days of
almost uninterrupted sunshine have made
us very dry. Daily waterings help to keep
things alive, but the grass is a little brown
in some parts of the lawns, and there are
yellow leaves on the Elms and the older

Laburnums. The dead dry leaves rustle so thick under foot in the Lime Avenue, that one looks up to see if any green is left.

Most of the German seed Grasses are already gathered, though a few have still to ripen. We always sow a good variety; they look so fresh while growing, and afterwards are dried for the winter. There is the pretty Tussock Grass, with soft downy tufts, and the long feathery kind, like waving hair; and one, most delicate and spray-like, is a sort of miniature Bulrush, with a green curved head; and then there is a little forest of our English Bashaw Grass (*Bromus aspen*). This is very handsome and gigantic in size, and came up of itself in one of the wild bits of the garden. The handsomest of all our Grasses this year is a fine blue Grass (Lyme Grass, *Elymus arenarius*), from the dunes of Holland. The colour amongst other greens is absolutely blue. It grows so strong, and the leaves so long, that it might almost be mistaken for an Iris. It is strange that this Grass should thrive apparently as well, or better, in a Buckingham-shire garden, than in its native sands! Near

the old Syringa (*Philadelphus*), on the turf at
the greenhouse door, two large pots of white
Campanula are stood out for change of air.
They are so tall that as one passes by in the
gloaming, one is startled by these tall white
people suddenly appearing out of the dusk.
Others of the same pyramidal Campanulas
remain in the house. They are pale pinkish
blue and white. Hundreds of blossoms
cover up and hide the whole plant, and
nothing is seen but the mass of wide open
flowerets. So cleverly are the flowers arranged, there is no sign of over-crowding
—and one asks how this is, for they seem to
be set quite close and even. " To questions
such as these Nature answers, ' I grow.' "
The Auratum Lilies had vainly promised to
open for so long that I almost lost patience.
The dry weather may have caused them to
delay. Constant watering seems now to
have begun to take effect, and there are
two or three superb blooms. The bulbs
are not taken up for the autumn ; they are
only covered over with fine ashes or cocoa-
nut fibre. If a plant will consent to live in
its own place winter and summer, it seems

so much more real, somehow. I wished to try the plan with our Spanish Irises, but in their case it proved a complete failure. Our large roots of Salvia Patens are seven years old; they are yearly cut down and covered with ashes.

The parterr is at this time in its full perfection. In other gardens I observe the blue Lobelia has done flowering, but our seedling that we raised, with bronze foliage, is as fine as it was two months ago. I cannot say the blue is so cool as the others, but the staying power of this special kind is of real importance, and the beds are most luminous. I am greatly enjoying a beautiful large blue Agapanthus in a green tub, placed on the grass near a trimmed Box tree, with a black Irish Yew for background. The scarlet Pelargoniums (must that long name be always said?) glow so hotly, they seem to want as much blue and green as we can give them. Never has our Magnolia Grandiflora flowered so well; I have counted nine great blossoms on the two trees at the same time. The texture of no other flower comes near to the beauty of the Magnolia. I remember long ago a white-chested beautiful boy, whose mother called him in play her Magnolia boy. That little child was the only flower I ever saw that could compare with the Magnolia!

SEPTEMBER.

13

"Time will not run back to fetch the age of gold."—MILTON.

"*In graceful succession, in equal fulness, in balanced beauty, the dance of the hours goes forward still.*"—EMERSON.

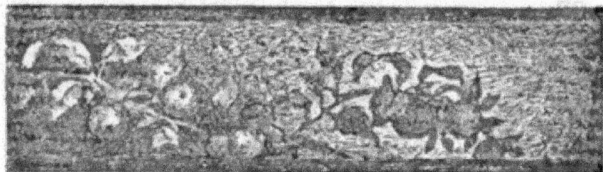

XII.

SEPTEMBER.

Of Psyche—Of an Old Garden—*Nil Desperandum*—
Of Branches bearing Beauteous Fruit.

September 17.—That is not to-day! Time
has since been sliding on faster and further
away from summer into autumn. Yet I
have a fancy to mark the date of as sweet
a September day as ever shone upon this
garden. I believe the people who got
most enjoyment out of the sunshine of that
marvellous day were the butterflies. There
was a real butterflies' ball held in the long
border of single Dahlias! An hour before
noon the flowers, beautiful in all the brilliance of their rainbow dyes, were visited
by a dancing throng of Atalanta butterflies.

Yellow, red, orange, lilac, white—every
flower had its Atalanta or two. They were
the finest butterflies of the kind I ever saw.
Strong on the wing, and faultless in the
perfection of their white-edged black velvet
and scarlet suits, they were the very embodi-
ment of joyousness. Not a jot did they care,
in their pride and joy of life, though a
hundred deaths surrounded them. They
knew nothing at all about that, indeed. Life
in the balmy air with the sunshine and the
flowers was all in all to them. A few shabby
Gamma moths, and hosts of humble bees,
combining business with amusement, mixed
in with the butterflies. By noon the whole
gay company dispersed. Later in the day
I found those fickle Atalantas disporting
themselves upon some yellow Everlastings
in another part of the garden. Butterfly
life varies in our garden year by year, but I
never saw so many Atalantas. This summer
we have seen few Peacocks or Tortoise-
shells. Orange-tips (*Euchlæ cardamines*)
were unusually plentiful in the spring, as
were also our White Cabbages throughout
the summer. So much fair weather as there

has been required a good supply! since two
white butterflies in the morning are the sure
sign of a fine day—and this summer they
had always to be about in pairs. Often,
a large brimstone has floated calmly by.
The chalkhill blue (*Polyommatus Corydon*),
for many past seasons noted as appearing about the Yew hedges in March, has
failed us this year; there have been no
humming-bird sphinxes, and the far-scented
Auratum Lilies, where often on warm evenings I have sought great Hawkmoths, seem
to have attracted nothing but scores of very
inferior-looking Gammas. It is an intense
pleasure to watch these various most beautiful beings, in all the freedom of their way-
ward wildness. No inducement would to
me seem powerful enough—now that the
barbarity of youth is past—to cause their
capture and death, were they never so rare
as specimens.

And now the rain and the falling leaves
recall but too vividly the true date (Sept. 28),
reminding me that I have to tell of the garden's autumnal desolation; yet if the days
would only keep fair and bright, enough still

is left there to make one happy. The single
Dahlias have won their way quite since last
I wrote, and now I love them dearly. They
are alone sufficient to light up half the
garden. Our chief border is made up of
seedlings, an exquisite variety of colours,
mauve or rose-lilac coming least often, and
a yellow with reddened or burnt-sienna
tipped petals by far the loveliest. Named
varieties are along with the Sunflowers
opposite. White Queen I like the best—
such large pure flowers. A White Queen
with an Atalanta butterfly settling on it
is a perfect little bit of contrasted colour.
I am schooling myself to say Dah-lia, but
habit is strong, and Daylia will persist in
coming out. In Curtis's *Botanical Magazine*
of 1803, vol. xix., p. 762, "Dahlia Coccinea,
scarlet-flowered Dahlia," is figured. There
is a note—"So named in honour of Andrew
Dahl, a Swedish botanist; . . . not to be
confounded with Dalea, a plant named after
Dale, the friend of Ray." The pronunciation
settled, the magazine goes on to say the
Dahlia is "a native of South America, and
may be considered as a hardy greenhouse

herbaceous perennial." These beautiful
flowers are especially valuable, since rain has
no effect on them, though rough winds so
easily break the brittle stems. The double
Dahlia is unknown in our garden ; it has
never been admitted. Fine as it is in form
and colour, the dislike to it seems, perhaps,
unreasonable, yet through some far-off association, I can never disconnect the double
Dahlia from a sort of mixture of earwigs
and pen-wipers! The clumps of Japanese
Anemones, both white and rosy-grey, are
full of an unfailing charm. We try to
prolong their existence by snipping off the
round seed-heads. One might as easily
make ropes of sand. . . . The same service
done to Dahlias is just within human possi-
bility. The dark red-mauve variety shows
an individuality which gives it great value in
the autumn borders. The irregularly shaped
flowers, whose narrow petals manifest an
inclination to double, last longer than those
of the other two kinds. Rain and wind have
destroyed the beauty of Salvia Patens ; it
will bloom out again, however. The rich
blue of this well-loved Salvia contrasts well

with white Anemones when mixed in the
flower-glasses. As for cut flowers, they are
always a doubtful pleasure. I gather them
with a pang, and would rather enjoy them
blooming their full time out in the garden.
And yet what other ornament is there—even
of finest porcelain—to compare with fresh-
cut flowers? Nor are pictures, nor rich
satins of Italy, sufficient without flowers to
make your room look bright and habitable.
Even that best decoration, walls well lined
with books, is the better for a few flowers
on the table. So that I am not yet prepared
to follow the example of the old lady who
never allowed one flower in her garden to
be cut, and filled her glasses with artificial
Roses! Sunflowers are sprouting round
their strong stems, and surrounded thus by
constellations of smaller suns, are perhaps
even handsomer than before. We have two
curiosities of Sunflower at this moment—
curious as demonstrating a resolve to exist
and flower under any circumstances whatever. One is a large thick-stemmed plant,
which must have met at some time with
some violent discouragement; it lies curled

round flat on the earth, looking almost like a poor starved cat with a large head; for, though quite overgrown with summer Phloxes and Roses, etc., one large flower at the end of its stalk tries to look up, while two or three of smaller size, growing along the stalk, do the same. In contrast to the deformity below it, a miniature Sunflower, slenderly graceful, with blossom no larger than a florin, springs out of the mortar between two bricks high up on the wall. There is no visible crevice, but some tiny nail-hole there must be where somehow a seed had lodged.

Though many borders have now begun to look forlorn, we feel the garden has done well. It is still quite full of flowers, in some parts gay, even, as it could never have been with the dulness of the most brilliant "bedding out." The entrance court is bright with Nicotiana, scarlet Pelargoniums, Zinnias, double white Petunia, and blue Lobelias. The long-desired pink China Roses, intended for these beds once, could not be found anywhere. Such simple loveliness is out of fashion, it seems! Torch plants (*Tritoma*)

are alight in all the edges of distant shrubberies. There are Japan Anemones and
Œnothera everywhere. The Sweet Pea
hedge by the tennis-court is out again in
bloom. Marigolds take care of themselves.
They keep going off and coming on again,
shining out in the dark where least expected.
Our Marigolds are of the deepest orange-
gold. The seed was brought from Cannes,
where their colour is always fine. They
incline to turn pale with us, so we have
to weed out pale faces in order to keep the
stock black-eyed and fiery. Golden Rod is
plentiful and useful, and I like it for the
sake of old remembrance. Eighty years ago,
as I used to hear, the gardens at Hampton
Court knew no other flowers at all.* The
great square beds were simply filled with
Golden Rod. Those must have been happier
days at Hampton Court, before carpet bedding was known—when the Yews were in
all their beauty, and the fountain sent up

---

* In the royal private gardens, however, at Hampton Court, rare plants were cultivated so far back
as 1691 ; such as the Green-flowered Knowltonia
Vesicatoria, etc.

its single lofty jet, and children played upon
the mimic harp wrought in the beautiful iron
gate of the Pavilion Walk, or peeped through
the bars at the browsing deer.

Amongst what may be called the ruck of
flowers throughout the garden, are deep
crimson Snapdragon, Zinnias, of all shades
of colour; Verbenas, pink, white, red, and
striped purple; low Phloxes, flesh-coloured
and crimson—more beautiful than they
ever were in their proper season; Musk,
Michaelmas Daisies, Euphea Platycentra,
Mignonette, Lobelias—the bronze-leaved
Lobelia Cardinalis; lilac and white and pink
Everlastings, white Marguerites and red
Pyrethrums, Princes' Feather, yellow Heartsease, and Mrs. Sinkins Pink in a grand
dash of second bloom—an endless variety,
all making the effort to put forth their best,
now that the last times draw so near. We
might gather baskets of flowers and fill the
house with them, were we so minded, and
still hardly miss them from the garden.
And yet has it not been said, " Bright tints
that shine are but a sign that summer's
past "? And full well I know the garden's

pleasure is even now growing towards
the end. Roses, it need scarcely be said,
abound; even Charles Lawson is red with
a second bloom. A few Damask Roses are
coming out by mistake. They look very
strange, putting one in mind of a long-for-
gotten Rose, the Rose des Quatre Saisons.
I see it clearly now, as I knew it in other
days—pink all over with its October blossoming—in a garden whose loveliness lives
only in the past. "Quarter Sessions" Rose,
the ancient guardian of the place not un
naturally used to say! Shall I try to paint
that garden? for surely none such exist any
more. It was like Shelley's poem of the
" Sensitive Plant," full of the poetry of trees,
and grass, and flowers. . . . A nearly level
space cut in the depths of a hanging wood;
no enclosing boundary to be seen, save here
and there, between the Rhododendrons, hints
of a mossy low stone wall, or the Sweet
Briar hedge at one end fencing off a stretch
of Cedarn turf. On the upper edge of the
gently sloping lawn a grand old Beech tree
with silvered bole caught the rays of the
morning sun. There was a giant Larch, all

bearded with long grey lichens; a Tulip tree,
a standard Magnolia. Here also was the
orangery; up its columns were twined
trumpet Honeysuckles and Passion-flowers.
In front, a sunny plot—oblong beds, with
narrow walks between—was devoted to
Carnations, Ranunculus, and many choicest
favourites. A walk wound round the lawn,
and upon the smooth grass were beds full of
lovely old-fashioned flowers. Large tree-
Roses, yellow Briars, and Scotch Roses (white
and red), and the old Queen of Sweden, and
tall poles covered with climbing Roses, loose-
petalled and cherry-coloured—Noissettes,
and Souvenir de Malmaison grew also on
the turf, with arches of Honeysuckle and
thickets of incense-breathing Spice plants.
On the lower shady side the walk went
on between bosquets of Kalmia and Azalea.
Here also great heaped-up limestone rock
formed a sort of natural wall between
the garden and the wood. Every cranny
was filled with rare and delicate Ferns and
all shade-loving Alpine plants, while double
white and blue Periwinkles streamed down
everywhere. Alpine Roses, too, flourished

here luxuriantly. On the lower side, at one corner, a vista was cut through the trees, so that over the Rhododendrons, here kept quite low, one looked through a frame of Beeches far away across the wide sunlit valley, across the corn and pastures, hedge-rows, coppice, and farm roofs, to the long range of wooded hills, and the grey tower cresting the distant headland. A little wire gate, hid behind the rocks, gave access to the garden from the house by a narrow path-way in the wood. I never knew that garden in its prime. When I remember it the sweetest flowers grew amid long weeds and grasses, and it had all the wild grace of a deserted garden ; for those who loved it were gone, and the old gardener could scarce hobble round to tend his " Quarter Sessions" Roses; and now he too is long dead, and the place is—modernized. . . .

The Fantaisie has been an unfrequented spot of late. It is a wilderness of flower and seeding plants, somewhat damp and overgrown. "The Forest" will have to be remodelled, and we contemplate an annexe on the north side. Such rapid growth is made that soon the character of both garden and Fantaisie must wholly change. The larger trees are fast losing that look of smiling youth which so enchants us in young newly planted wood. Each little tree is growing tall, and each begins to spread itself in uncompromising isolation. Evergreens encroach more and more upon the borders, crowding out the flowers and crowding each other, so as to render necessary many a painful sacrifice. Twelve months ago signs of the coming change were hardly visible. Since regret is unavailing, new plans must be laid to draw new pleasures from the inevitable. I note with some pride that the experiment of beheading Cryptomeria Elegans succeeds so far that in every instance the trees bush out healthily, instead of running up into brown raggedness.

As I write, near the library window, a dim glory seems to be stealing round. The light from a stormy sunset has fired the Virginian Creeper and the apples on a large tree beyond the stone ball at the corner of the wall. The leaves glow blood-red, and the fruit shines like molten ore. The tree is decaying, with a huge brown fungus feeding on its heart. It is so old that a Virginian Creeper was planted to grow up the gaunt trunk, and Mistletoe is left to flourish over all the branches as it lists. Yet in a good apple year the fruit still clusters from the top of the tree down almost to the ground. And growing on its green lawn thus, one dreams a passing dream of the apples of the Hesperides, and the red Virginian climber is the great fiery scaled dragon gliding up through the leaves to gaze with dull eye seawards. But there are no maidens dancing in a ring, and I have just seen three hungry thrushes attack the apples unforbidden.

Nothing is so uncertain as pears. There has been a first-rate lot on a young Flemish Beauty, growing against the Gardener's cottage. They have been gathered earlier than usual, which may be the reason why they surpass in flavour and juiciness those of last year. Williams' Bon Chrétien, always good, is this year somewhat impaired in outward appearance by black dots all over the fruit. Can these dots be caused by the age of the

trees ? In one half of the Vine-houses long
bunches of white Muscats are hanging still.
They are crisp and finely flavoured, and
show well against a purple background of
Madresfield Court. Next season we hope
for a crop of Frontignacs, to satisfy the
wish for old-fashioned thin-skinned Grapes.
Round the windows the Vines are yellowing,
with green fruit ripening fast. These are
unusually sweet for outdoor Grapes, and
have yielded a fair wine in their time.
Large green Apples (*Reinette du Canada*),
in the walled garden, are nearly as beauti-
tiful as the trees of Blenheim Orange which
are reddening in the orchard.

Very pleasant and Arcadian in the mellow
autumn sunshine are these days of Apple
gathering! There is no undue haste; the
man on the ladder up in the tree leisurely
fills his basket. Baskets, half full of fruit,
stand near, upon the leaf-strewn grass.
Children are sure to gather round, and
there is, an odour of ripe Apples upon the
air. After an indecision of some years'
duration, I have at last arranged my
September bill of fare—in Arcadia !—Grapes

14

and Pears to look at, Nectarines and "the curious Peach" to smell, fresh Figs to feed on in the morning, Golden Drop Plums all day long!

But, ah! there has chanced just now a golden drop of quite another kind. The last gold sand has fallen of the last hour of these dear garden days, and only one more word must be said—Farewell!

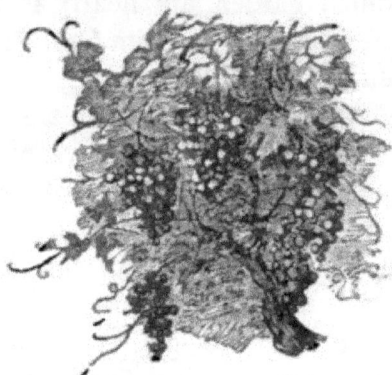

MARK TIME DOST THOU

www.ingramcontent.com/pod-product-compliance
Lightning Source LLC
Chambersburg PA
CBHW030318270326
41926CB00010B/1418